Learning Web-based Virtual Reality

Build and Deploy Web-based Virtual Reality Technology

Srushtika Neelakantam

Tanay Pant

Apress®

Learning Web-based Virtual Reality: Build and Deploy Web-based Virtual Reality Technology

Srushtika Neelakantam
Bangalore, Karnataka, India

Tanay Pant
Ghaziabad, India

ISBN-13 (pbk): 978-1-4842-2709-1
DOI 10.1007/978-1-4842-2710-7

ISBN-13 (electronic): 978-1-4842-2710-7

Library of Congress Control Number: 2017935381

Managing Director: Welmoed Spahr
Editorial Director: Todd Green
Acquisitions Editor: Pramila Balan
Development Editor: Matthew Moodie
Coordinating Editor: Prachi Mehta
Copy Editor: Kim Wimpsett
Compositor: SPi Global
Indexer: SPi Global
Artist: SPi Global
Cover image designed by Freepik

Distributed to the book trade worldwide by Springer Science+Business Media New York, 233 Spring Street, 6th Floor, New York, NY 10013. Phone 1-800-SPRINGER, fax (201) 348-4505, e-mail orders-ny@springer-sbm.com, or visit www.springeronline.com. Apress Media, LLC is a California LLC and the sole member (owner) is Springer Science + Business Media Finance Inc (SSBM Finance Inc). SSBM Finance Inc is a **Delaware** corporation.

For information on translations, please e-mail rights@apress.com, or visit www.apress.com/rights-permissions.

Apress titles may be purchased in bulk for academic, corporate, or promotional use. eBook versions and licenses are also available for most titles. For more information, reference our Print and eBook Bulk Sales web page at www.apress.com/bulk-sales.

Any source code or other supplementary material referenced by the author in this book is available to readers on GitHub via the book's product page, located at www.apress.com/978-1-4842-2709-1. For more detailed information, please visit www.apress.com/source-code.

Printed on acid-free paper

To my beloved parents, and my brother,
without whom none of my success would be possible.

—Srushtika Neelakantam

To my parents, who gave me the dream.

—Tanay Pant

Contents at a Glance

About the Authors.. xi

Acknowledgments xiii

■Chapter 1: Introduction to VR and WebVR 1

■Chapter 2: Bringing VR to the Web and
WebVR Frameworks 5

■Chapter 3: Setting Up Your VR Lab and Popular
WebVR Projects 11

■Chapter 4: Introduction to A-Frame... 17

■Chapter 5: From "Hello, World" to a VR Content Display 39

■Chapter 6: Building a VR-Based Movie Theater............................ 53

■Chapter 7: A-Frame Components and the Registry 63

■Chapter 8: Version Control and Deploying Your Code
on GitHub 69

Index.. 81

Contents

About the Authors.. xi

Acknowledgments xiii

■Chapter 1: Introduction to VR and WebVR 1

Introducing Virtual Reality 1

Types of VR Hardware Setup 2

Web-Based Virtual Reality 3

    Opportunities for WebVR Applications 3

    Current State of WebVR 4

Virtual Reality Devices Available in the Market 4

Summary.. 4

■Chapter 2: Bringing VR to the Web and WebVR Frameworks 5

The WebVR API 5

What Is MozVR?.. 6

Is Your Browser WebVR Enabled?.. 6

WebVR Developer Tools 6

    A-Frame.. 6

    WebVR-Boilerplate.. 8

    Vizor... 8

Summary.. 9

■**Chapter 3: Setting Up Your VR Lab and Popular WebVR Projects** **11**

Google Cardboard 11

Oculus Rift 13

HTC Vive 14

Other Requirements 14

A-Painter 15

Blair Witch WebVR Experience 15

    Quake 3 WebGL Demo 16

Summary 16

■**Chapter 4: Introduction to A-Frame 17**

Introducing the A-Frame Library 17

    A Simple Example 18

    A Basic Application 18

    Key Features of A-Frame 19

The Entity-Component System 20

    Caching Assets to Improve Performance.. 21

    Mixins 21

    Components and Building Blocks of A-Frame 21

Primitives 22

    <a-box> 22

    <a-camera> 23

    <a-cursor> 23

    <a-circle> 24

    <a-collada-model> 25

    <a-cone> 26

    <a-curvedimage> 26

<a-cylinder> 27

<a-dodecahedron> 28

<a-image> 28

<a-light> 29

<a-obj-model> 29

<a-octahedron> 30

<a-plane> 30

<a-ring> 31

<a-sky> 31

<a-sound> 32

<a-sphere> 32

<a-tetrahedron> 33

<a-torus> 33

<a-torus-knot> 34

<a-video> 34

<a-videosphere> 35

A-Frame Inspector 35

Scene Graph 36

Viewport 36

Components Panel 37

Summary 38

■Chapter 5: From "Hello, World" to a VR Content Display 39

Building a Simple "Hello, World" VR Application 39

bm-font-text-component 39

Understanding the Flow of the Application 40

Building a VR Content Display Web Site 45

Summary 52

■**Chapter 6: Building a VR-Based Movie Theater**............................ **53**

Planning the Movie Theater.. 53

Building 3D Models with MagicaVoxel 60

Getting Prebuilt Models from Clara 61

Summary.. 61

■**Chapter 7: A-Frame Components and the Registry** **63**

Components in A-Frame.. 63

Lifecycle Methods of Components 64

    Component.init()... 64

    Component.update().. 64

    Component.remove().. 64

    Component.tick()... 64

    Component.pause() and Component.play()... 64

Built-in Components... 65

Using A-Frame Registry Components 66

Summary.. 68

■**Chapter 8: Version Control and Deploying Your
Code on GitHub** **69**

Introduction to Version Control Systems 69

Advantages of Version Control 70

Git: All You Need to Know 71

    Git vs. GitHub... 72

    Installing Git on Your Machine 72

Working with GitHub... 73

Hosting Your VR Web Site for Free Using GitHub Pages 77

Summary.. 79

Index.. **81**

About the Authors

Srushtika Neelakantam (https://srushtika.github.io) is a student in computer science major at Sir M. Visvesvaraya Institute of Technology, Bangalore. She is a tech speaker at Mozilla and has spoken at various national and international tech conferences. She is a developer for the Android and web platforms. She runs a learning club in Bangalore where she actively advocates for an open Web and teaches web literacy to the people in her region. She is a Mozilla representative and actively contributes to the Mozilla VR project. She's part of the Campus Advisory Committee, which aims at making contributions to Mozilla's open source projects easier for students.

Tanay Pant (https://en.wikipedia.org/wiki/Tanay_Pant) is an Indian author, speaker, hacker, innovator, and tech enthusiast. He is best known for his work on various books about computer science, his open source contributions, and his talks at technology conferences. He is the chief architect of Stock Wolf (www.stockwolf.net), a global virtual stock-trading platform that aims to impart practical education about stocks and markets. He is also an alumnus of the Mozilla Representative Program, and you can find his name listed in the credits (www.mozilla.org/credits/) of the Firefox web browser. You can also find articles written by him on web development at SitePoint and TutsPlus.

Acknowledgments

Srushtika Neelakantam: I'd like to thank the Apress team, for their guidance throughout publishing my first book; Ms. Pramila Balan and Ms. Prachi Mehta, for patiently handling all my impatient queries; and all the other people at Apress, secretly and silently involved with this book.

Thanks to Sri Krishnadevaraya Trust, the management of my college; to my principal, Dr. M.S. Indira, for always supporting me; to my professors and mentors at my university, Mr. Dilip. K. Sen and Dr. VijayaKarthik, who've always steered me in the right direction and provided me with the right resources to achieve what I wanted; and to all my teachers throughout my life—I have had so many wonderful things to learn from each one of you!

Thanks to Mr. Kevin Ngo and Mr. Ram Dayal Vaishnav, for introducing me to virtual reality and WebVR—the journey has been amazing ever since, with your guidance. Thanks also to Mr. Shivagangadhar Kolli, for introducing me to Mozilla in my early days of college; to Ms. Havi Hoffman, for introducing me to MozTechSpeakers and giving me the opportunity to learn new technologies; to my mentor at Mozilla, Ms. Konstantina Papadea, for helping me with every possible thing and providing me with the right resources I needed to complete this book; and to my longtime friends, B.S Archana, Athira Girish, Vineel Reddy, Galaxy Kadiyala, Harsha Vardhan, Santosh Vishwanatham, Akshay Tiwari, Sumanth Damarla, and all my well-wishers, for always inspiring me and supporting me in all my endeavors.

Thanks to my extended family, which consists of so many amazing people who are always ready to share useful things and opportunities with me - you know who you are! To my father, Mr. Manmohan Raju, for always supporting me in all my endeavors; to my mother, Mrs. Vani Priya, for always nagging me to do the right thing; and to my amazing little brother, Mr. Srujan Raj, for always inspiring me to learn new things.

Tanay Pant: I would like to express my warmest gratitude to the many people who saw me through this book and to all those who provided support, read, wrote, assisted, and offered their insights. I would like to thank my family for their huge support and encouragement. Thank you to my father, who always inspired me to do something different, something good, with my life. I could not have asked for a better role model in my life! I am grateful to my mother, who has been the biggest source of positivity and a pillar of support throughout my life.

I would like to thank Donovan Kraeker (drawvr.com) for his code contributions in Chapter 6. I want to thank Apress for enabling me to publish this book and the Apress team for providing smooth passage throughout the publishing process! I also would like to thank the professors at the College of Technology – Pantnagar, who provided me with the support I needed to write this book.

■ ACKNOWLEDGMENTS

Thank you to Dr. H. L. Mandoria, Dr. Ratnesh Prasad Srivastava, Er. Sanjay Joshi, Er. Rajesh Shyam Singh, Er. B.K. Pandey, Er. Ashok Kumar, Er. Shikha Goswami, Er. Govind Verma, and Er. Subodh Prasad, for your motivation. My deepest gratitude to all the teachers who taught me from kindergarten through engineering. Last but not the least, my thanks and appreciation go to all my friends and well-wishers, without whom this book would not have been possible.

Thank you!

CHAPTER 1

■ ■ ■

Introduction to VR and WebVR

In this chapter, you will improve your understanding of virtual reality (VR) and web-based virtual reality by studying the various techniques you can use to build a virtual environment as well as web-based virtual reality. We will also cover why a web developer should learn the various WebVR frameworks, the current state of WebVR, and finally the various VR devices available for purchase in the market.

Introducing Virtual Reality

Virtual reality is basically a set of technologies and computer hardware that, when combined, are used to create an immersive simulation of a three-dimensional environment. The virtual environment is usually a replication of a real environment and is achieved using three-dimensional settings (such as depth perception), sounds, and instruments such as consoles to allow users to interact with it. The movement of a user is tracked using either a head-mounted apparatus or using motion detection sensors.

Virtual reality is used in a lot of fields such as video games, engineering, education, psychological therapy, e-commerce, marketing, and art. For example, virtual reality is used in third-person games to provide a realistic digital environment for gamers to interact with separate from the real world. In both engineering and education, mechanical modeling using computer-aided design (CAD) software allows engineers and students to manipulate and develop the models they have designed as if they were working with a physical object.

Recently Samsung released a video on YouTube that showed people wearing VR headsets trying to stabilize themselves on the edge of high-rise buildings. These types of activities are used in psychological therapies. In this case, VR was helping people overcome acrophobia. In another example, VR allows users to browse through virtual stores and handle the objects they intend to purchase. This allows e-commerce web sites to market their products in an effective way. Finally, Tilt Brush by Google truly awed the world when it was first introduced. It allows users to paint with virtual paintbrushes in a three-dimensional environment using two hand consoles. This enables artists to create virtual pieces of art, which can be printed later using a three-dimensional printer.

© Srushtika Neelakantam and Tanay Pant 2017
S. Neelakantam and T. Pant, *Learning Web-based Virtual Reality*,
DOI 10.1007/978-1-4842-2710-7_1

Types of VR Hardware Setup

There are primarily two basic types of hardware setups for experiencing a virtual reality.

- *Computer-connected*: In a computer-connected VR setup, position sensors and a high-resolution head-mounted display (HMD) are connected to a computer system, and the various VR equipment uses the computer system for processing jobs (see Figure 1-1).

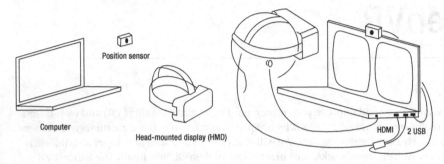

Figure 1-1. *Computer-based VR setup*

- *Mobile-based*: A mobile-based VR setup consists only of the HMD and is constructed with the help of a smartphone, which acts as the display as well as providing sound output. It uses a VR mount, which holds the smartphone and contains the lens to impart stereoscopic vision to the user. Unlike headsets with integrated displays that are used in computer-connected virtual reality devices, these units are essentially enclosures that a smartphone can be inserted into (see Figure 1-2).

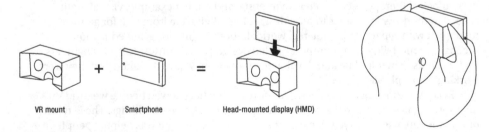

Figure 1-2. *Mobile-based VR setup*

Web-Based Virtual Reality

First conceived in the spring of 2014 at Mozilla, WebVR is an experimental JavaScript application programming interface (API) that provides support for a large variety of virtual reality devices via a web browser. WebVR is easy to experience because it works seamlessly on most smartphones in such a way that a user's experiences begin and end in a web browser. You can just send a link to someone to share your web-based WebVR experience with them.

The WebVR API is an amazing addition to any web developer's toolkit. It allows you to develop simulated environments using HTML5, CSS3, and JavaScript. Unlike with devices such as Microsoft HoloLens and Oculus Rift, you do not need any special software development kit (SDK) to develop VR applications or games.

With the various WebVR frameworks that have been developed, the complexity of leveraging WebGL efficiently and writing huge chunks of JavaScript code has been eliminated. You can now develop basic WebVR applications with just HTML5 as a prerequisite, and the WebVR frameworks abstract away all the complicated work for you. Using WebVR, you can create applications that run across a wide variety of platforms. In addition, virtual reality experiences are accessible to users irrespective of the processing power of the device because WebVR helps adjust the experience to the best that the device can handle. This means that even low-end devices can still provide a decent VR experience.

If your browser does not support WebVR (say you're running Safari on your Mac), you can simply use your mouse to move your "virtual head," or your field of view, and use the WASD keys for moving your character (if the developer has enabled this functionality). Hence, you can easily debug, test, and have fun developing WebVR applications even if you have no hardware required for running WebVR applications.

Opportunities for WebVR Applications

With the release of economical and easily accessible VR mounts such as Google Cardboard, the number of users trying VR technologies has been rising sharply. WebVR applications do not require any special hardware for a user; they require just a smartphone and VR mount. In addition, WebVR treats HTML5 as a first-class citizen, so it's easy for web developers to turn regular web sites into VR experiences.

Web sites contain a lot of data such as pictures, videos, API streams, and text, and web developers have found ways to display all this information in a neat and concise way using different web frameworks and libraries. Now, WebVR offers the chance to display all these pieces of information in a realistic and impressive way in a VR environment.

For example, pictures can be displayed as portraits in a virtual art gallery. Text can be displayed as a billboard, and the data from API streams can be dynamically used to generate messages written on a notice board. All these different components can be simulated realistically in a virtual environment. These are just some examples of what can be achieved. Developers can totally revolutionize the way users experience web sites and interact with them.

3

Current State of WebVR

There are lots of WebVR frameworks that you can employ to get started with your first web-based virtual reality experience; they will be covered in Chapter 2. There are also many decent visual editors for constructing VR scenes, which will help you with professional WebVR development. Chapter 3 covers many popular projects that have been developed using the available frameworks that will inspire you to jump-start development using WebVR frameworks. These frameworks are being actively developed, and new features are being added for developer communities every day. This is turning WebVR into a huge sensation with sophisticated tools available for developing an incredible product. The browser development teams are also evolving quickly to adapt to the growing VR landscape.

Virtual Reality Devices Available in the Market

Virtual reality devices that can display immersive virtual environments are available for purchase from many companies all over the world. HTC Vive, Oculus Rift, Sony PlayStation VR, Samsung Gear VR, Google Cardboard, Google Daydream View, Microsoft HoloLens, Razer OSVR HDK 2, Fove VR, Sulon Q, OnePlus Loop VR, LG 360 VR, Zeiss VR One, Avegant Glyph, Zeiss VR One GX, and Homido are some of the most popular computer-connected and mobile-based virtual reality devices available in the market.

Of these virtual reality devices, only Samsung Gear VR has Super AMOLED display along with a proximity sensor. (AMOLED stands for "active-matrix organic light-emitting diode.") In Chapter 3, we will discuss which devices are best for economically practicing the exercises given in the book.

Summary

In this chapter, you learned about virtual reality, types of hardware setups for VR devices, web-based virtual reality, the need to develop applications utilizing web-based virtual reality, and the current state of WebVR. You then learned about the various devices that can run virtual reality environments available in the market.

In the next chapter, you will learn about the WebVR API and briefly look at the W3C specifications for the WebVR API. You will also learn about MozVR and the various WebVR frameworks that are used by WebVR developers (and that we will be using in this book). You will also learn about the efforts being made by various browsers to support WebVR.

■ ■ ■

CHAPTER 2

Bringing VR to the Web and WebVR Frameworks

In this chapter, you will learn more about the WebVR API and quickly look at the W3C specifications for it. You will also learn about MozVR and the various WebVR frameworks that are used by WebVR developers (and that we will be using in this book). You will also learn about the efforts being made by various browsers to support WebVR with the help of MozVR's online application.

The WebVR API

The WebVR API is an experimental JavaScript API that provides access to virtual reality devices such as Oculus Rift, HTC Vive, Samsung Gear VR, and Google Cardboard via a web browser. This API is currently available in the nightly builds of Firefox, in the experimental builds of Chromium, and in Samsung Internet for Gear VR. The Editor's Draft of the WebVR specification has been posted on GitHub (https://w3c.github.io/webvr/) by the World Wide Web Consortium. This specification describes support for accessing virtual reality devices, including sensors and head-mounted displays, via the Web. It is a pretty long document. You should try giving it a read if you are interested in contributing to these open source browser projects and to the development of WebVR frameworks. However, if it seems too dry, you can skip it. We'll walk you through some of the WebVR API specification from a high-level view in this chapter.

Hardware that enables VR applications requires high-precision and low-latency interfaces to deliver decent and lag-free experiences. We already discussed in Chapter 1 that WebVR also aims to provide a decent experience for lower-end devices. Other interfaces, such as device orientation events, can be repurposed to become VR input, but doing so dilutes the interface's original intent and often does not provide the precision necessary for high-quality VR. The WebVR API provides purpose-built interfaces to VR hardware, which allows developers to build realistic and comfortable VR experiences.

The best place to get involved in contributing to WebVR is the WebVR mailing list (https://mail.mozilla.org/listinfo/web-vr-discuss). Another great place to interact with WebVR enthusiasts is the WebVR Slack channel (https://webvr.slack.com). Developers of these browsers as well as a lot of expert community members hang around this channel, so it is a great place to get started.

© Srushtika Neelakantam and Tanay Pant 2017
S. Neelakantam and T. Pant, *Learning Web-based Virtual Reality*,
DOI 10.1007/978-1-4842-2710-7_2

What Is MozVR?

MozVR stands for the Mozilla Virtual Reality team; this team works on including and improving support for WebVR in the Firefox web browser as well as developing the A-Frame WebVR framework. MozVR's web site (`https://mozvr.com`) consists of information on getting started with WebVR for various devices such as iOS and Android (using VR mounts), Oculus Rift, and HTC Vive. It also has an amazing gallery of demos that have been built with WebVR technologies.

Is Your Browser WebVR Enabled?

If you want to know which features of WebVR are supported by which browser, then you can make use of MozVR's "Is WebVR Ready?" web site (`https://iswebvrready.org`). This web site helps you obtain information on specific features and figure out whether they run on a given browser. It also provides information on the state of development of these features as well as information on how they can be enabled in case they aren't enabled by default in a browser.

The web site also provides information on the implementation of features such as the WebVR API, Oculus Rift support, HTC Vive support, the Gamepad API, Gamepad extensions, Gamepad haptics, Gamepad pose, Gamepad touchpad support, the Web Audio API, and the Web Speech API.

WebVR Developer Tools

In the previous chapter, we discussed the current state of WebVR. We'll now discuss some of the frameworks and tools that are available for constructing an effective and amazing virtual reality experience for the Web. Please note that the intention of this section is just to get you familiar with the various tools and frameworks. Hence, this is only a brief introduction to get you excited about the stuff that is available for developers. You will be learning about some of these frameworks and tools in future chapters to build your WebVR applications and will be studying them more in depth at that time.

A-Frame

A-Frame (`https://aframe.io/`) is an open source WebVR framework that is being developed by the MozVR team for creating virtual reality experiences with HTML (see Figure 2-1). You can build VR scenes that work across a wide variety of smartphones, desktops, Oculus Rift, and HTC Vive. It basically encapsulates the complicated WebGL and JavaScript code and allows you to build virtual reality scenes using just HTML. A-Frame is a three.js framework, and it works on the entity-component system pattern that we will cover more in Chapter 4. A-Frame drastically reduces the boilerplate code and has been classically crafted for web developers. It also provides a fallback for experiencing the same content without requiring a VR device.

Figure 2-1. *A-Frame*

A-Frame is by far the best framework for developing web-based virtual realities; it is also one of the fastest-evolving frameworks in this genre. There are some awesome demo projects, along with their source code, showcased on A-Frame's web site. A-Frame also has an inspector that can be used to move around objects in a scene and manipulate them. This inspector is essentially like a what-you-see-is-what-you-get (WYSIWYG) editor for WebVR scenes that you have written using the A-Frame library. This is a relatively new addition to A-Frame's functionalities, and you will learn how to effectively use the editor along with the rest of the framework in Chapter 4.

Figure 2-2 shows the default example scene opened in the online editor of the A-Frame inspector. The various components of the scene appear on the left, and you can view the scene from different angles. You can manipulate the objects in a three-dimensional environment (with an *x*-, *y*-, *z*-axis system).

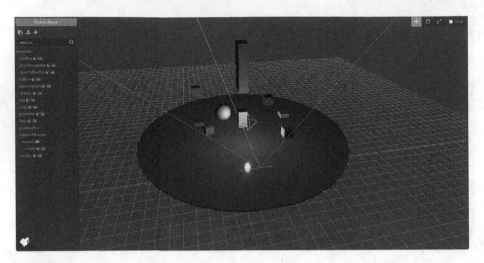

Figure 2-2. *Online editor of A-Frame*

WebVR-Boilerplate

WebVR-Boilerplate (`https://github.com/borismus/webvr-boilerplate`) is a three.
js-based starting point for web-based virtual reality experiences. This project uses webvr-
polyfill, which is a JavaScript implementation of the WebVR specifications. webvr-polyfill
lets you view the same content if you do not have a virtual reality viewer. A-Frame uses
webvr-boilerplate and webvr-polyfill.

This project basically acts as a "getting started" example and provides a reasonable
user experience for getting in and out of virtual reality and "magic window" modes.

Vizor

Vizor (`http://vizor.io/`) is an online platform for creating and publishing web-based
virtual reality content. Vizor allows you to discover three-dimensional content in virtual
reality on your phone or in two dimensions in your web browser or on your tablet. Vizor
has a list of tutorials on its blog (`http://blog.vizor.io`), which will help you get started
with Vizor.

Vizor's editor window has lots of features. It also has many prebuilt three-
dimensional models that you can include in your VR scene. It offers options to program
these models to add animations, group them with other models, or add them under a
hierarchy of models. There is also an option to chat with fellow community members,
which allows you to ask for help and get feedback quickly. Vizor also allows you to
publish the VR scenes that you have developed on its web site.

Figure 2-3 shows the default layout of Vizor in Build mode.

Figure 2-3. *Vizor in Build mode*

Summary

In this chapter, you learned about the WebVR API and took a look at the W3C specification for the WebVR API. You also learned about MozVR, the browsers that are WebVR enabled, and the various WebVR frameworks and tools that are used by WebVR. You also learned about the efforts being made by various browsers to support WebVR with the help of MozVR's online application.

In the next chapter, you will learn about the various hardware and software requirements to continue with WebVR application development. You will then learn to set up and run WebVR applications on Oculus Rift and Google Cardboard. Finally, you will learn about the popular WebVR projects available online to get inspired by so you can go on to build your own WebVR project.

Summary

■ ■ ■

CHAPTER 3

Setting Up Your VR Lab and Popular WebVR Projects

In this chapter, you will learn about the various hardware and software requirements to continue with WebVR application development. You will then learn how to set up and run WebVR applications on Oculus Rift and Google Cardboard. Finally, you will learn about some popular WebVR projects available online to get inspired by so you can go on to build your own WebVR project.

Google Cardboard

Google Cardboard is a virtual reality mount that is intended for use with smartphones. It has been so named because it can be constructed using the specifications published by Google using cardboard as the body of the VR mount. This platform is intended as a low-cost system to increase interest and encourage developers to start building VR applications. If you are not interested in building this yourself, you can purchase a prebuilt Google Cardboard mount from any e-commerce store like Amazon. The cost of the device will vary with the quality of the material that has been used to build the body of the mount as well as the lenses. For example, a VR mount made of plastic is going to cost more than a mount made of cardboard. Google Cardboard is the most economical option available if you have a smartphone.

Let's get started with Google Cardboard! First, you need to install a WebGL-compatible web browser on your smartphone. The more processing power your phone has and the faster it is, the better. A-Frame should work properly with mobile Safari for iOS, Firefox for iOS, Firefox for Android, and Chrome for Android. If you are using an iPhone, please make sure you have iOS 9.1 or greater so that the examples will work.

To start, open the web browser on your smartphone and go to A-Frame's web site. Our favorite demo is the Anime UI one (https://aframe.io/examples/showcase/anime-UI/). Open it and change your phone's orientation to landscape mode to get a better view of the VR scene. Move your phone around and you will notice that the field of view of the VR landscape changes. It looks like Figure 3-1.

© Srushtika Neelakantam and Tanay Pant 2017
S. Neelakantam and T. Pant, *Learning Web-based Virtual Reality*,
DOI 10.1007/978-1-4842-2710-7_3

Figure 3-1. *A-Frame Anime UI demo*

There are some things worth noticing here. First, notice that even though you are viewing the demo in landscape orientation on a mobile screen, the movement of the various components in the scenery with respect to each other give the whole scene a three-dimensional look. The next thing you might notice is that your view of the scene changes as fast as you move the smartphone. This demonstrates that the field of view changes are tied to the accelerometer of your mobile device. Finally, notice that there is a small VR icon on the bottom right of the screen.

This is the magic button that upon clicking will split the screen of the landscape into two in such a way that each part of the screen fits in front of the individual lenses of Google Cardboard for stereoscopic vision, which will help you in perceiving the WebVR scene in 3D. You just have to open your Google Cardboard mount, fit the phone inside the contraption, and seal the opening of the cardboard. Make sure you have carefully stabilized your smartphone inside the cardboard and securely sealed up the VR mount. You can now wear the Google Cardboard mount and experience the amazing VR scene that was constructed using just HTML.

Figure 3-2 shows what the Anime UI scene looks like after you activate VR mode by clicking the VR icon on the bottom right of the smartphone screen.

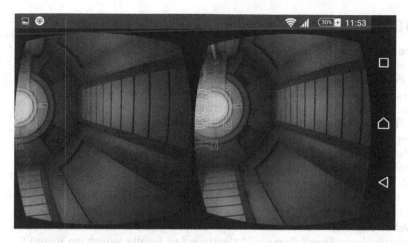

Figure 3-2. Anime UI, VR mode

In the examples, we will be running all the WebVR applications that build in future chapters in Google Cardboard for testing purposes. However, you can feel free to run your applications in other VR mounts or devices such as Oculus Rift or HTC Vive.

Oculus Rift

Oculus Rift is a computer-connected virtual reality device that comes with a head-mounted display and sensors called *constellation* and *controllers*. To use WebVR with your Oculus Rift device, first you have to install the latest Oculus runtime (https://developer3.oculus.com/downloads/). After that, you need to install either Firefox Nightly or an experimental build of Chromium. Please note that Mac and Linux devices are not supported by Oculus Rift and hence cannot be used for viewing WebVR content. Ensure that your Oculus settings allow for unknown sources.

Once you have followed these steps, open A-Frame's web site for viewing WebVR content. Finally, click the Enter VR button to send content to the Oculus Rift headset. You are now all set to experience WebVR content and use Oculus Rift to run and test the applications that you will be building in later chapters of this book.

HTC Vive

HTC Vive is another computer-connected VR device; it has been developed by HTC and Valve Corporation. Vive comes with sensors, an HMD, and controllers. To use WebVR content with Firefox on Vive, you first need to install the Firefox Nightly version. Then, download version 1.02 of the openvr_api.dll file from the OpenVR GitHub repository (https://raw.githubusercontent.com/ValveSoftware/openvr/master/bin/win64/openvr_api.dll). Next, save the openvr_api.dll file somewhere on your computer where the user running Firefox can read it. In Firefox Nightly, navigate to about:config and change the value of dom.vr.openvr.enabled to true and the value of gfx.vr.openvr-runtime to the full path of the openvr_api.dll file. Finally, you need to restart Firefox Nightly to be able to enjoy your WebVR content.

To run with the Chromium web browser, first install an experimental build of Chromium. Then, in the address bar, load chrome://flags#enable-webvr and toggle the Enable WebVR flag. Now, load chrome://flags#enable-gamepad-extensions in the address bar and toggle the Enable Gamepad Extensions flag. Finally, launch the SteamVR application and view the WebVR content.

Other Requirements

Once you have managed to get your hands on a VR device for testing and execution, you can start to assemble the software requirements that you will have in order to build web-based virtual reality applications. First, you will need a web browser. You can use any browser that is mentioned at IsWebVRReady.org.

In addition, we will be using Git for version controlling our WebVR applications. To install Git, download the appropriate package for your operating system from https://git-scm.com/downloads. To test whether Git has been correctly installed on your operating system, open your terminal, type git, and you should see the following output:

```
Tanays-MacBook-Air:~ tanay$ git
usage: git [--version] [--help] [-C <path>] [-c name=value]
           [--exec-path[=<path>]] [--html-path] [--man-path] [--info-path]
           [-p | --paginate | --no-pager] [--no-replace-objects] [--bare]
           [--git-dir=<path>] [--work-tree=<path>] [--namespace=<name>]
           <command> [<args>]

-----snip-----
```

You will also be learning to push your codebase to GitHub and deploy your WebVR applications using GitHub Pages. That is all you'll need in this book to start WebVR application development.

Let's now take a look at some of the amazing projects that have been built by people and organizations using WebVR technologies so you can get an idea of what is possible using WebVR.

A-Painter

A-Painter is a Google Tilt–like creation developed by the MozVR team that allows you to paint in virtual reality in your browser. To get started with A-Painter, head to the A-Painter web site (`https://aframe.io/a-painter/`). To run this project locally, type the following commands in your console:

```
git clone git@github.com:aframevr/a-painter && cd a-painter npm install
npm start
```

The project should now be up and running at `http://localhost:8080` in your browser. Please note that currently only the experimental Chromium build on Windows supports the Vive controllers. (You will need to enable these flags for WebVR and the Gamepad extensions: `chrome://flags#enable-webvr` and `chrome://flags#enable-gamepad-extensions`.)

Blair Witch WebVR Experience

The Blair Witch WebVR experience (`www.blairwitch.com/experience/`) is a pretty scary and exciting simulation of the events related to the horror movie *The Blair Witch Project*. This demo (Figure 3-3) gives you ideas, not to mention goosebumps, about what kind of interactive environments you can develop to make your WebVR a memorable experience.

Figure 3-3. *Blair Witch WebVR experience*

Quake 3 WebGL Demo

Quake 3 WebGL Demo (http://media.tojicode.com/q3bsp/) is a mock-up of the classic game *Quake 3* (Figure 3-4). This demo gives you an idea of what is possible using WebGL, WebVR, and artistic thinking.

Figure 3-4. *Quake 3 WebGL Demo*

Summary

In this chapter, you learned about the various hardware and software requirements for getting started with WebVR application development. You then learned to set up and run WebVR applications on Oculus Rift and Google Cardboard. Finally, you learned about some popular WebVR projects to get inspired by so you can start thinking about your own WebVR projects.

In the next chapter, you will learn about the A-Frame library for WebVR development. Specifically, you'll learn how to use the various components and building blocks of A-Frame, cache assets for better performance, apply textures to objects, control the lighting and cameras, and run WebVR applications on your system.

CHAPTER 4

■ ■ ■

Introduction to A-Frame

In this chapter, you will learn about the A-Frame library for WebVR development. Specifically, you'll learn how to use the various components and building blocks of A-Frame, cache assets for better performance, apply textures to objects, control the lighting and cameras, and run WebVR applications on your system.

Introducing the A-Frame Library

The Mozilla VR team developed A-Frame (Figure 4-1) in mid-2015. A-Frame is a WebVR framework that makes implementing virtual reality experiences quicker and easier by letting you code with HTML without having to know the powerful yet complex WebGL. It is open source, and the VR scenes that you can build using the A-Frame library work across smartphones, desktop computers, and most other VR devices. The Mozilla VR team's goal was to interest mainstream web developers in the WebVR ecosystem. With A-Frame, 3D virtual reality content can be easily manipulated by designers, web developers, and a lot of other communities that do not have any experience with WebGL.

Figure 4-1. *This is the A-Frame logo that includes a simple illustration of 3D objects*

© Srushtika Neelakantam and Tanay Pant 2017
S. Neelakantam and T. Pant, *Learning Web-based Virtual Reality*,
DOI 10.1007/978-1-4842-2710-7_4

A-Frame comes with the basic building blocks of virtual reality scenes such as models, skies, cursors, animations, and so on. The already available templates for some basic scenes make it easier for a web developer to get started.

You implement A-Frame in HTML with a special tag called <a-scene> that holds all the VR content.

A Simple Example

Before coding the content for your virtual reality scene, you need to include the JavaScript build script in the <head> tag of the HTML document.

The easiest way to do this is to include the JavaScript build from the content delivery network (CDN), as follows:

```
<!-- Production Version, Minified -->
<script src="https://aframe.io/releases/0.3.2/aframe.min.js"></script>
<!-- Development Version, Uncompressed with Source Maps -->
<script src="https://aframe.io/releases/0.3.2/aframe.js"></script>
```

You can also download the JavaScript build to serve it locally.

- https://aframe.io/releases/0.3.2/aframe.min.js: Minified version
- https://aframe.io/releases/0.3.2/aframe.js: Uncompressed version with source maps

A Basic Application

The following is a simple "Hello, World" application using the A-Frame library (the result is shown in Figure 4-2):

```
<!DOCTYPE>
<html>
  <head>
        <script src="https://aframe.io/releases/0.2.0/aframe.min.js"></
script>
  </head>
  <body>
        <a-scene>
                <a-box color="#4CC3D9" width="2" height="1" depth="2"
position="0 5 0" scale=" 1 2.5 1">
                </a-box>
                <a-sky color="#ECECEC"></a-sky>
        </a-scene>
  </body>
</html>
```

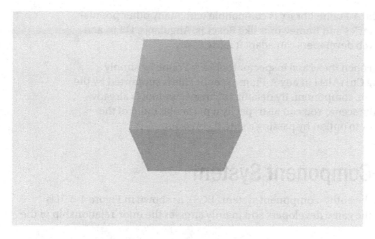

Figure 4-2. *"Hello, World" application in a browser*

Here's an explanation of the other code:

- *The <a-scene> tag*: The complete content of the VR web site that you are building will be contained inside this HTML tag. Apart from being a container, it doesn't have any other specific function.

- *The <a-box> tag*: This is a box primitive that displays a simple box. We will discuss this in detail later in this chapter.

- *The <a-sky> tag*: The 360-degree sphere background of a virtual reality scene is called a *sky* and can be specified using the <a-sky> tag. Either it can be a plain color, which can be specified using a hex code, or it can be a 360-degree image (also referred to as an *equirectangular* image).

Hence, for the previous example, you start with the basic structure of the HTML document. Then, inside the <head> tag, you add a reference to the JavaScript dependency. Within the <body> tag, you add a special tag called <a-scene>, as described in the previous list, and include all the contents of the VR web site in it.

Key Features of A-Frame

HTML is one of the easiest-to-write languages used on the Web, and virtual reality's association with HTML makes VR all the more usable for many developer communities. These are some key features of A-Frame:

- Boilerplate code is a piece of code that has to be included in many places through an application with little or no alteration at all. A-Frame completely replaces the boilerplate code associated with WebVR with a single tag: <a-scene>.

- Since the A-Frame library is compatible with many other popular web libraries and frameworks like React.js, Angular.js, D3.js, and so on, web developers can adapt it fairly easily.

- You can open the visual inspector tool in A-Frame by simply pressing Ctrl+Alt+I in any A-Frame scene. This is supported by the inspector component. By default, the inspector tool is already set on the scene. You can also specify a particular build of the inspector to option by passing a URL if you want.

The Entity-Component System

A-Frame is built on the entity-component system (ECS), as shown in Figure 4-3. It is commonly used by the game developers and mainly stresses the inter-relationship of the components.

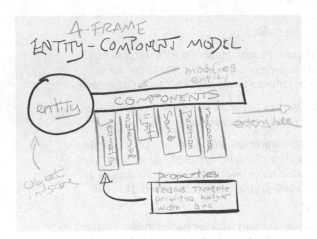

Figure 4-3. *Kevin's illustration of the entity-component system*

An *entity* is a generic placeholder that has no functionality by itself, but it allows you to associate various components with it in order to render their necessary appearance and functionality. Components add the specific details to the entities they are plugged into. A system manages a similar group of components and provides them with the necessary services.

Figure 4-3 shows a rough sketch by Kevin Ngo, a VR developer who works on A-Frame. The ECS framework allows developers to tack on various plug-and-play components and to create their own components with customized attributes.

Caching Assets to Improve Performance

The asset management system of A-Frame is a powerful tool that allows you to place all assets in a single place. Additionally, the assets stored and used via the asset management system have an added advantage over those included traditionally within the individual components/entities. These assets are preloaded when the web site is launched and are cached for better performance during run time.

You identify an asset management system with the <a-assets></a-assets> tags, within which you place all the assets. The following are the various assets supported by the asset management system:

- <a-asset-item>: This can be a miscellaneous and infrequently used asset like a custom 3D model.

- <audio>: This includes the audio files.

- <img>: This includes the images.

- <video>: This includes the videos.

The virtual scene is completely blocked until all the assets that are included in a particular HTML file either are fetched or error out.

Mixins

You use mixins to declare some frequently used component attributes. The components can later use and remix one or more of these mixins. The mixins always have an ID as an attribute, and the components access the mixins by their IDs.

```
<a-scene>
 <a-assets>
  <a-mixin id="black" material="color: black"></a-mixin>
  <a-mixin id="green" material="color: green"></a-mixin>
  <a-mixin id="ball" geometry="primitive: sphere"></a-mixin>
 </a-assets>
 <a-entity mixin="black sphere"></a-entity>
 <a-entity mixin="green sphere"></a-entity>
</a-scene>
```

The mixins are declared directly in the <a-assets> tag, as shown in the previous code. Essentially, the mixins represent all the attributes that a particular entity should contain. This way, it becomes easier to reuse the same kind of attributes in many entities, without having to write them each time.

Components and Building Blocks of A-Frame

As explained earlier, a component is just a pile of data that describes the attributes of an entity. You use these attributes to modify the appearance and functioning of the entity. For instance, a car is an entity, and the number of gears, horsepower, and so on, are its attributes.

In A-Frame, a component can be registered and configured to an entity, as shown here:

```
<a-entity geometry="primitive: sphere; radius: 5"
          light="type: point; color: crimson; intensity: 2.5"
          position="5 0 0">
</a-entity>
```

You can think of components for entities as analogous to CSS for HTML.

A lot goes on behind the scenes for these components. For instance, consider the position component from the previous code. It is implemented as follows, which looks fairly complex. However, this component can be readily used on the fly.

```
AFRAME.registerComponent('position', {
  schema: { type: 'vec3' },
  update: function () {
    var object3D = this.el.object3D;
    var data = this.data;
    object3D.position.set(data.x, data.y, data.z);
  }
});
```

Primitives

Primitives have a semantic name such as <a-box>. They are the entities that have their components preset with some default attribute values. Such primitives help map the component properties with the HTML values. They act as shorthand tools to simplify the common entities that are otherwise complex to implement.

The <a-entity> tag is extended by all the primitives, and because of this, all the operations that can be implemented on the <a-entity> tag can also be implemented on the primitives, such as specifying position, adding animation, attaching components and mixins, and so on.

The primitives API allows you to easily specify certain entities by directly using the respective tag and enlisting the other appearance and behavior attributes.

Let's now take a look at the various primitives offered by the A-Frame.

<a-box>

This is the simplest of all the primitives. You can use the box primitive to create a box (cube, cuboid, bricks, and so on) of any size and color (Figure 4-4). Additionally, like any other primitive, the box can be made to rotate or animate in a certain way by specifying the respective attributes.

```
<a-box color="blue" depth="1" height="1" width="1"></a-box>
```

Figure 4-4. *A box*

You can also specify a texture to be used on the box. To do this, just add the PNG texture image in the assets, specify an ID for it, and use the src attribute of the <a-box> tag to specify it, as shown here:

```
<a-assets>
 <img id="texture" src="linepattern.png">
</a-assets>
<a-box src="#texture"></a-box>
```

<a-camera>

You can use the camera primitive to specify a particular position in the scene where the user will be initially taken. For instance, if you have a scene with a box placed on the roof of a room, you can use the camera primitive to position the initial view of the scene such that the box is in the view area. To do this, you specify the position in terms of x-, y-, and z-coordinates in the 360-degree sphere of the VR scene. By default, the camera is placed at 0, 1.6, 0 in desktop mode and 0, 0, 0 in VR mode.

```
<a-camera position="0 7 5">
</a-camera>
```

<a-cursor>

The cursor primitive implements the click feature so that the user can interact with the scene. By default it has a ring geometry (Figure 4-5) and is usually added as an immediate child to the <a-camera> tag. It works a little differently than the traditional cursors since there is no click button on a VR device or controller. With <a-cursor>, you can specify the wait time before the click action is initiated. After the specified time elapses, the element present at the position of the cursor is clicked.

```
<a-camera>
        <a-cursor></a-cursor>
</a-camera>
```

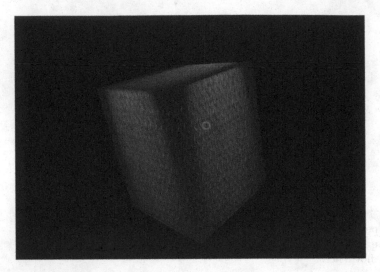

Figure 4-5. *The box primitive with a camera and cursor entity for triggering rotation*

The cursor primitive has an attribute named fuse-timeout, which c an be used to set the wait time (in milliseconds) for the cursor before it can trigger a fuse-based click event. If not specified, it takes a default value of 1500.

<a-circle>

The circle primitive is similar to the box primitive. It creates a circular plane on the VR scene (Figure 4-6).

```
<!-- Basic circle. -->
        <a-circle color="red" radius="10"></a-circle>
        <!-- Textured circle parallel to ground. -->
        <a-circle src="#platform" radius="20" rotation="-70 10
0"></a-circle>
```

Figure 4-6. *The circle primitive in a browser*

You can make a circle parallel with the ground by rotating it around the x-coordinate and keeping the y- and z-coordinates at 0.

<a-collada-model>

The word *collada* refers to collaborative design activity. This primitive allows you to use the 3D Collada models available on the Web or created using modeling software (Figure 4-7). You can simply include the model in the assets and refer to it using the src attribute of this primitive.

```
<a-scene>
            <a-assets>
                    <a-asset-item id="thor" src="thor.dae">
            </a-assets>
        <!-- Using the asset management system. -->
        <a-collada-model src="#thor"></a-collada-model>
 <!-- Defining the URL inline. Not recommended but more comfortable for web
developers. -->
        <a-collada-model src="thor.dae"></a-collada-model>
</a-scene>
```

Figure 4-7. *A sample Collada model*

\<a-cone\>

The cone primitive is used to create a 3D cone shape in a VR scene (Figure 4-8). Some of the key attributes include the height and the radius, as shown here:

```
<a-cone color="tomato" radius-bottom="2" radius-top="0" height="5"
position="-15 0 4">
</a-cone>
```

Figure 4-8. *The previous code snippet displays this cone*

\<a-curvedimage\>

The curved image primitive is used to curve the usually flat images to make them more relevant to be included in a 360-degree VR scene. Visually, it looks like the image is pasted onto the surface of a cylinder.

```
<a-curvedimage id="pana" src="#panorama-demo" transparent="true" height="2"
radius="3" theta-length="40" rotation="0 190 0" position="0 0 -2">
</a-curvedimage>
```

Sometimes, the image is distorted when stretched inappropriately (Figure 4-9). To avoid this, be careful when specifying the attribute values with respect to the image's aspect ratio.

Figure 4-9. A curved image that is distorted because of an incorrect aspect ratio

<a-cylinder>

You can use the cylinder primitive to create 3D cylinders for implementing pipes and curved surfaces (Figure 4-10).

```
<a-cylinder color="crimson" height="3" radius="1.5"></a-cylinder>
```

Figure 4-10. The a-cylinder primitive in a browser

27

<a-dodecahedron>

A dodecahedron is a three-dimensional model with 12 equal pentagonal faces (Figure 4-11). This model can be implemented easily using the dodecahedron primitive.

```
<a-dodecahedron color="green" radius="10"></a-dodecahedron>
```

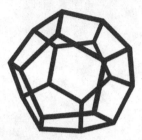

Figure 4-11. *A dodecahedron in a browser*

<a-image>

The image primitive is used to include flat-plane images as opposed to curved ones (Figure 4-12).

```
<a-image src="another-image.png"></a-image>
```

Figure 4-12. *a-image primitive with a color attribute*

An image can have a color attribute that can be used to give color to an image, in which case it looks just like a 2D plane.

<a-light>

The light primitive is used to adjust the lighting in the A-Frame scene (Figure 4-13). There can be two types of lighting types: point and ambient. As you can see from their names, they implement the respective lighting in the scene.

```
<a-light type="point" color="blue" position="0 5 0"></a-light>
```

Figure 4-13. *a-light illustration on a box primitive*

<a-obj-model>

Wavefront Technologies has built an advanced visualizer package, which is a 3D graphics software package used in many sci-fi movies. The geometry definition of .OBJ is a 3D model format for creating and sharing the 3D models.

Such 3D models can be included in a VR scene by using the obj-model primitive. Each such model has two files, the .obj and .mtl files. Figure 4-14 shows one such 3D model.

```
<a-obj-model src="boat.obj" mtl="boat.mtl"></a-obj-model>
```

Figure 4-14. *An example of a 3D model*

\<a-octahedron\>

An octahedron is a 3D model with eight equal triangular faces (Figure 4-15). This can be easily implemented in a VR scene using the octahedron primitive.

```
<a-octahedron color="#FF926B" radius="5"></a-octahedron>
```

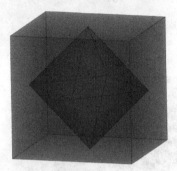

Figure 4-15. *An octahedron*

\<a-plane\>

You can use the plane primitive to create a flat surface in a VR scene (Figure 4-16).

```
<a-plane src="#ground" height="100" width="100" rotation="-90 0
0"></a-plane>
```

Figure 4-16. *a-plane primitive*

<a-ring>

You can use the ring primitive to create either a ring shape or a filled disc shape, as shown in Figure 4-17.

```
<a-ring src=="#lifesaver" radius-inner="1" radius-outer="2"></a-ring>
```

Figure 4-17. *An a-ring*

<a-sky>

As explained earlier, the sky primitive allows you to add a 360-degree image as a background to a particular VR scene. These images are readily available on the Internet; alternatively, you can create a 360-degree image by using Google's 360-degree camera application (Figure 4-18).

```
<a-assets>
            <img id="sky" src="sky.png">
    </a-assets>
    <a-sky src="#sky"></a-sky>
```

Figure 4-18. *An example of a 360-degree image*

A 360-degree image renders perfectly as a sphere when used with the sky primitive.

\<a-sound\>

The sound primitive is really interesting because it allows you to wrap some sounds within your VR scene.

```
<a-sound src="src: url(click.mp3)" autoplay="true" position="0 2
5"></a-sound>
```

The sound primitive is best experienced in VR games. It adds to the other effects for a better experience.

\<a-sphere\>

The sphere primitive is different from the circle primitive in just the usual geometry. The sphere primitive implements a 3D ball object with the required color or pattern (Figure 4-19).

```
<a-sphere src="#disco" radius="5" position="0 15 5"></a-sphere>
```

Figure 4-19. *a-sphere primitive used with a disco-ball image in the src attribute*

<a-tetrahedron>

As the name suggests, this primitive can be used to create a tetrahedron model in a VR scene (Figure 4-20). A tetrahedron is a polyhedron that consists of four equal triangular faces.

```
<a-tetrahedron color="#FF926B" radius="5"></a-tetrahedron>
```

Figure 4-20. *A tetrahedron*

<a-torus>

Love donuts? A torus (Figure 4-21) is the shape for you. This primitive implements a donut-shaped object in a VR scene.

```
<a-torus color="#43A367" arc="270" radius="5" radius-tubular="0.1">
</a-torus>
```

Figure 4-21. *a-torus primitive in a browser*

<a-torus-knot>

A torus knot, as shown in Figure 4-22, implements a pretzel-shaped model.

```
<a-torus-knot color="#B84A39" arc="180" p="2" q="7" radius="5"
radius-tubular="0.1"></a-torus-knot>
```

Figure 4-22. *A torus-knot primitive*

<a-video>

The video primitive allows you to include a video to be played on a flat screen inside the VR scene.

```
<a-video src="backgroundvideo.mp4"></a-video>
```

\<a-videosphere\>

The videosphere primitive is interesting in the sense that it plays the video on the surface of a 360-degree sphere, analogous to the sky of the scene (Figure 4-23).

```
<a-videosphere src="spherevid.mp4"></a-videosphere>
```

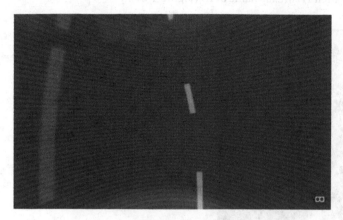

Figure 4-23. a-videosphere output in a browser

A-Frame Inspector

The A-Frame inspector is a useful visual tool that allows developers to inspect the A-Frame scene and make minor changes to it using a graphical user interface (GUI).

The inspector offers the following facilities:

- You can resize, reposition, and rotate the entities present in the scene using the handles.

- Widgets allow you to tweak the properties of entities and their components.

- You can visually observe the changes in attribute values in the scene without having to switch between the code editor and the browser.

Activate the inspector by pressing Ctrl+Alt+I. This shortcut opens the particular scene in the inspector after having fetched its code via the CDN. You can use the same shortcut to close the inspector and return to the scene.

You can use the inspector for any A-Frame scene unless the developer of the scene has explicitly disabled it.

The A-frame inspector consists of the components covered in the following sections.

Scene Graph

The scene graph of the A-Frame inspector is a hierarchical tree structure of the scene's elements. You can use the scene graph to clone, add, delete, search for, and select the entities or to export HTML.

As the A-Frame scene is primarily coded in HTML, the entities present in the scene graph are displayed using their HTML tag name or ID (Figure 4-24).

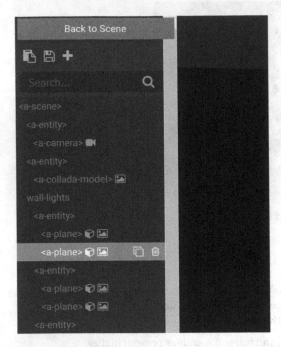

Figure 4-24. *Entities in the scene graph*

Viewport

The viewport is the most interesting component of the inspector (Figure 4-25). It displays the scene along with all the scales, dimensions, positions, and so on. You can rotate, zoom, or even pan the view in the viewport in order to check the scene from different angles and distances.

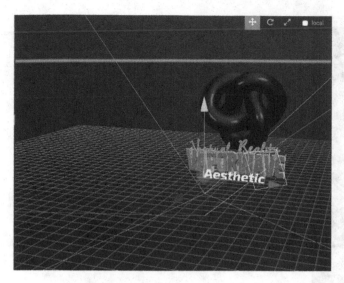

Figure 4-25. *Viewport*

Additionally, the viewport allows you to select the individual entities and transform them. This can be implemented as follows:

- *Select*: Click the entity either directly from the viewport or from the scene graph.

- *Transform*: Transforming an entity means changing the size and/ or position of the entity in the scene, visually. After selecting the required entity, choose one of the helper tools (translate, rotate, scale, or local) and drag one of the three axis coordinates (represented by red, blue, and green) around the entity to apply the particular changes.

Components Panel

The components panel shows the components and attributes of the entity selected (Figure 4-26). It allows you to modify the common component values of the entities used. Each attribute might have the same or different widgets as the others.

Figure 4-26. *Components panel*

This provides an excellent way to visually enhance the A-Frame scene after setting up its basic layout. After you are satisfied with the visual representation with certain values, you can copy the HTML output of individual components so that you can reuse them in the source code in later scenarios.

Summary

In this chapter, you got a basic introduction to the A-Frame library along with the key concepts necessary for its use. Next, you learned about the entity-component system. You saw a way to cache the resources used in the A-Frame project in order to readily load up the scene without any delay. You then learned about the various primitives offered by A-Frame and checked how to use the inspector to check and tweak these scenes with little effort.

The key to mastering A-Frame is to experiment with all these primitives in various scenes so you can get a visual feel about how each component works.

In the next chapter, you will build a "Hello, World" VR application using A-Frame followed by a 3D web site based on VR, from scratch.

■ ■ ■

CHAPTER 5

From "Hello, World" to a VR Content Display

In this chapter, you will build a simple "Hello, World" application using A-Frame. After that, you will build a simple content web site similar to an image gallery but with an added virtual reality experience.

Building a Simple "Hello, World" VR Application

In this section, you'll get your hands dirty on your first-ever piece of code in A-Frame. As is customary with many frameworks or languages people learn, you'll print "Hello, World!" in an A-Frame VR scene.

Before we start, we'll discuss an A-Frame component called bm-font-text-component, which you'll use to print the text in the VR scene. You'll study more about components in Chapter 7.

bm-font-text-component

bm-font-text-component is a ready-to-use A-Frame component that allows you to add some text in a specified font and set other desired properties. It displays text and a bitmap in A-Frame using signed distance field rendering (see Figure 5-1).

© Srushtika Neelakantam and Tanay Pant 2017

S. Neelakantam and T. Pant, *Learning Web-based Virtual Reality*,
DOI 10.1007/978-1-4842-2710-7_5

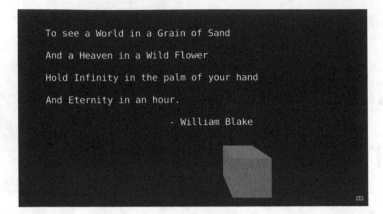

Figure 5-1. *Displayed using bm-font-text-component*

Figure 5-1 shows the default font; however, you can specify any custom font you'd like. Other most commonly used properties include the width of the text box, alignment, color, opacity, and so on. Like any other component in the VR scene, this text does not appear to be on a flat screen, but it gently spreads itself to appear to be curved.

To implement bm-font-text-component directly in your code, you need to include the following JavaScript in the header of your HTML:

```
<script src="https://rawgit.com/bryik/aframe-bmfont-text-component/master/
dist/aframe-bmfont-text-component.min.js"></script>
```

Understanding the Flow of the Application

We'll now cover everything that you'll include in your first VR application.

The VR scene you will make will be Earth as seen from a satellite, with the sun in the backdrop. You'll use a simple box to add some animation, and you'll also focus some light on this box. Next, you'll add the text "Hello, World!" in the default font in front of this rotating box. Additionally, you'll put a grid over Earth to represent the hypothetical location coordinates.

So, the whole thing comes down to an astronaut greeting the world with that message! Can't imagine the scene yet? No problem. Let's get started and things will become understandable soon.

Let's quickly set up the initial skeleton of the HTML document, complete with the script references required and the <a-scene> tag.

```
<html>
  <head>
    <script src="https://aframe.io/releases/0.3.2/aframe.min.js"></script>
    <script src="https://rawgit.com/bryik/aframe-bmfont-text-component/
master/dist/aframe-bmfont-text-component.min.js"></script>
  </head>
```

```
<body>
  </a-scene>
  </a-scene>
</body>
</html>
```

Now that you have the basic skeleton in place, let's add the `<a-assets>` tag inside the `<body>` tag, which will include all the resources you'll use for the scene. Initially, let's include the image to be used as the sky in the scene; Figure 5-2 shows the image.

```
<a-assets>
        <img id="sky" src="images/sunrise.jpg"  />
</a-assets>
```

Figure 5-2. sunrise.jpg

You can find this image and all the other offline resources used in this book in this Flickr repository: `https://www.flickr.com/gp/136974235@N05/90538e`.

Next, let's add the grid on Earth like a sphere that appears when `sunrise.jpg` is used as the sky. This will represent the hypothetical latitude and longitude location lines.

```
<a-assets>

        <img id="sky" src="images/astrosky.jpg" crossorigin="anonymous" />
    <img src="https://img.gs/bbdkhfbzkk/stretch/https://i.imgur.com/25P1geh.
png" id="grid" crossorigin="anonymous">

</a-assets>
```

Next, update the `<a-scene>` contents to include the sky and the grid.

```
      <a-scene>
      <a-entity position="0 -10 0" geometry="primitive: plane;
width: 10000; height: 10000;" rotation="-90 0 0" material="src: #grid;
repeat: 10000 10000; transparent: true;metalness:0.6; roughness: 0.4;
sphericalEnvMap: #sky;">
      <a-entity>
<a-sky src="#sky" rotation="0 -90 0"></a-sky>
<a-scene>
```

In all the entities, you include an attribute called sphericalEnvMap that defines the spherical environment map for the particular entity. Because you already have a sky set up, you'll refer it to the particular resource.

The VR scene now looks like Figure 5-3.

Figure 5-3. *VR scene*

If yours doesn't look like this, go back to the code and check for inconsistencies or errors.

Now you'll add a simple component, a 3D box, to try the animation and light feature.

```
<a-entity scale="4 4 4" geometry="primitive: box;" position="0 4 -10"
material="color: #c5b2a0; metalness:1; roughness: 0.3; sphericalEnvMap:
#sky;">
<a-animation easing="linear" attribute="rotation" dur="10000" to="0 0 360"
repeat="indefinite">
</a-animation>
</a-entity>
```

You can also use the <a-box> primitive to implement this box. Since you have already learned how to use that primitive, try it now.

Note the animation primitive included inside the box entity. The attributes are pretty much self-explanatory. While implementing this, try changing the values of all the attributes to understand how the scene changes with different values.

Next, throw some light on the box to add some drama and make the sun's light more realistic and match better with the environment.

```
<a-entity light="color: white; intensity: 0.5" position="-5 5
15"></a-entity>
```

The position of all the entities follows the x-, y-, and z- coordinate strategy. Play with these in the inspector or manually experiment with different values to understand the perspective.

The scene should now look like Figure 5-4.

Figure 5-4. *The scene now*

You'll now add the final and most important part of this A-Frame scene: the text.

```
<a-entity scale="5 5 5" bmfont-text="text: HELLO WORLD!; size: 1.5; height:
0.5;" position="-1 3 -7"></a-entity>
```

The complete "Hello World" scene looks like Figure 5-5, and Listing 5-1 shows the complete consolidated code.

Figure 5-5. *The "Hello World" example*

You should experiment with different attribute values for each entity and component used.

Listing 5-1. index.html

```
<html>
  <head>
    <script src="https://aframe.io/releases/0.3.2/aframe.min.js"></script>
    <script src="https://rawgit.com/bryik/aframe-bmfont-text-component/
    master/dist/aframe-bmfont-text-component.min.js"></script>
  </head>
  <body>

        <a-assets>
        <img src="https://img.gs/bbdkhfbzkk/stretch/https://i.imgur.
com/25P1geh.png" id="grid" crossorigin="anonymous">
        <img src="https://img.gs/bbdkhfbzkk/2048x1024,stretch/http://i.
imgur.com/WMNH2OF.jpg" id="chrome" crossorigin="anonymous">
        <img id="sky" src="images/astrosky.jpg" crossorigin="anonymous" />
        </a-assets>

    <a-scene>
      <a-entity scale="5 5 5" bmfont-text="text: HELLO WORLD !; size: 1.5;
      height: 0.5;" position="-1 3 -7"></a-entity>

    <a-entity scale="4 4 4" geometry="primitive: box;" position="0 4 -10"
material="color: #c5b2a0; metalness:1; roughness: 0.3; sphericalEnvMap:
#sky;">
```

```
        <a-animation easing="linear" attribute="rotation" dur="10000" to="0
0 360" repeat="indefinite"></a-animation>
    </a-entity>

    <a-entity position="0 -10 0" geometry="primitive: plane; width: 10000;
height: 10000;" rotation="-90 0 0" material="src: #grid; repeat: 10000
10000; transparent: true;metalness:0.6; roughness: 0.4; sphericalEnvMap:
#sky;">
    </a-entity>

    <a-entity light="color: white; intensity: 0.5" position="-5 5 15">
    </a-entity>

    <a-sky src="#sky" rotation="0 -90 0"></a-sky>

    </a-scene>
  </body>
</html>
```

Building a VR Content Display Web Site

In this section, you'll develop a content display web site in VR. Essentially, you'll build
a photo gallery of four tourist destinations around the world, shown with curved
thumbnails. If one of those thumbnails is clicked, the whole sky turns into that image
as if you were standing in that spot. You will also include some basic JavaScript for
implementing the functionality.

We'll use the <a-curved-image> primitive for the thumbnails. Let's begin with the
basic HTML skeleton along with the a-scene tag and a sky. All the offline resources are
available in the Flickr repo at https://www.flickr.com/gp/136974235@N05/v4JeEp.

```
<html>
    <head>
        <meta charset="utf-8">
        <title>Let's go places</title>
        <script src="./js/aframe.min.js"></script>
    </head>
    <body>
        <a-scene auto-enter-vr>
          <a-sky id="sky" src="Images/grid1.svg" color="rgb(200,200,200)" >
    </a-sky>
        </a-scene>
    </body>
</html>
```

Figure 5-6 shows the scene so far.

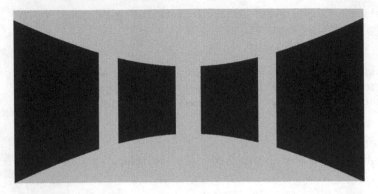

Figure 5-6. *Scene so far*

Next, following the usual flow, let's add the images as assets.

```
<a-assets>
        <img id="horseshoe" src="Images/horsethumb.jpg">
        <img id="switzerland" src="Images/switzerlandthumb.jpg">
        <img id="bc-place" src="Images/bcplacethumb.jpg">
        <img id="atlanticocean" src="Images/atlanticthumb.jpg">
</a-assets>
```

Next, you add these as curved image primitives inside the `<a-scene>` tag, as follows:

```
<a-curvedimage id="swit" src="#switzerland" transparent="true"
    height="2" radius="3" theta-length="40" rotation="0 240 0" position="0 0 -2">
</a-curvedimage>

<a-curvedimage id="curhorseshoe" src="#horseshoe" transparent="true"
    height="2" radius="3" theta-length="40" rotation="0 190 0" position="0 0 -2">
</a-curvedimage>

<a-curvedimage id="atlantic" src="#atlanticocean" transparent="true"
    height="2" radius="3" theta-length="40" rotation="0  130 0" position="0 0 -2">
</a-curvedimage>

<a-curvedimage id="bc" src="#bc-place" transparent="true"
    height="2" radius="3" theta-length="40" rotation="0  80 0" position="0 0 -2">
</a-curvedimage>
```

If you use these same resource files, your VR scene should now look like Figure 5-7.

Figure 5-7. *The VR scene so far*

The text that you see on the thumbnails is not a text component but part of the image. So, don't worry if you have not found the text component in the code yet.

In an A-Frame scene, the cursor can be implemented using a camera entity. It needs to have a shape and a default position. It will be used to implement the click functionality. To let the user know that the click is being applied, you will add some animation to this cursor.

In this case, you will make the cursor to be a ring shape, which shrinks in size to demonstrate a click function. You'll link this click function to the JavaScript code that will change the sky primitive to some predefined image, depending on the thumbnail clicked. The camera entity is implemented as follows:

```
<a-entity>
            <a-entity camera look-controls wasd-controls>
                <a-entity position="0 0 -3" scale="0.2 0.2 0.2"
                geometry="primitive: ring; radiusOuter: 0.20;
                radiusInner: 0.13;" material="color: #ADD8E6; shader:
                flat" cursor="maxDistance: 30; fuse: true">
                    <a-animation begin="click" easing="ease-in"
                    attribute="scale" fill="backwards" from="0.1 0.1
                    0.1" to="1 1 1" dur="150"></a-animation>
                    <a-animation begin="fusing" easing="ease-in"
                    attribute="scale" fill="forwards" from="1 1 1"
                    to="0.2 0.2 0.2" dur="1500"></a-animation>
                </a-entity>
            </a-entity>
</a-entity>
```

The VR scene with the camera entity should now look like Figure 5-8; observe the small blue ring-shaped element in the center of the scene. That is the cursor.

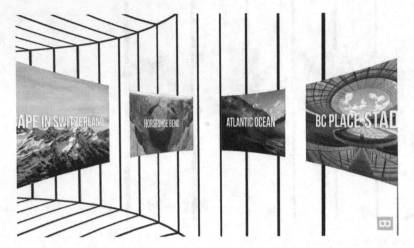

Figure 5-8. *The cursor*

Now, it's time to add the JavaScript. You can include JavaScript in many ways. In this example, you will include it in the body of the HTML right after ending the `<a-scene>` tag.

```
<script>
            document.querySelector("#curhorseshoe").
            addEventListener('click', function() {
                document.getElementById("sky").
                    setAttribute("src","Images/Horeshoe-Bend-PS.jpg");
            });
            document.querySelector("#atlantic").addEventListener('click',
            function() {
                document.getElementById("sky").
                    setAttribute("src","Images/atlantic.jpg");
            });
            document.querySelector("#swit").addEventListener('click',
            function() {
                document.getElementById("sky").
                    setAttribute("src","Images/switzerland.jpg");
            });
            document.querySelector("#bc").addEventListener('click',
            function() {
                document.getElementById("sky").
                    setAttribute("src","Images/bc-place.jpg");
            });
</script>
```

The document.querySelector selects an entity with the specified ID. Using this, you get the ID of the particular curved image that is clicked by the user. Next, you need to add an event listener to each of these selectors to identify the different curved images present in the scene.

Inside the event listener, you get the sky primitive using the ID mentioned in the <a-sky> tag. Next, you use the setAttribute method to set the attribute named src equal to some value, which in this case is a path or link to the image you want to apply as the sky.

You repeat this for every curved image thumbnail and set the respective images to be the sky on a click. See Figures 5-9 and 5-10.

Figure 5-9. *Sky changed to "Landscape in Netherlands" image*

Figure 5-10. *Sky changed to "Horseshoe Bend" image*

Listing 5-2 shows the complete consolidated code.

Listing 5-2. VR content display Web Site

```
<html>
    <head>
        <meta charset="utf-8">
        <title>Let's go places</title>
        <script src="./js/aframe.min.js"></script>
    </head>
    <body>
        <a-scene auto-enter-vr>
            <a-assets>
                <img id="horseshoe" src="Images/horsethumb.jpg">
                <img id="switzerland" src="Images/switzerlandthumb.jpg">
                <img id="bc-place" src="Images/bcplacethumb.jpg">
                <img id="atlanticocean" src="Images/atlanticthumb.jpg">
            </a-assets>

            <a-entity>
                <a-entity camera look-controls wasd-controls>
                    <a-entity position="0 0 -3" scale="0.2 0.2 0.2"
                    geometry="primitive: ring; radiusOuter: 0.20;
                    radiusInner: 0.13;" material="color: #ADD8E6; shader:
                    flat" cursor="maxDistance: 30; fuse: true">
                        <a-animation begin="click" easing="ease-in"
                        attribute="scale" fill="backwards" from="0.1 0.1
                        0.1" to="1 1 1" dur="150"></a-animation>
                        <a-animation begin="fusing" easing="ease-in"
                        attribute="scale" fill="forwards" from="1 1 1"
                        to="0.2 0.2 0.2" dur="1500"></a-animation>
                    </a-entity>
                </a-entity>
            </a-entity>

            <a-curvedimage id="swit" src="#switzerland" transparent="true"
              height="2" radius="3" theta-length="40" rotation="0 240 0"
              position="0 0 -2">
            </a-curvedimage>

            <a-curvedimage id="curhorseshoe" src="#horseshoe"
            transparent="true"
              height="2" radius="3" theta-length="40" rotation="0 190 0"
              position="0 0 -2">
            </a-curvedimage>

            <a-curvedimage id="atlantic" src="#atlanticocean"
            transparent="true"
              height="2" radius="3" theta-length="40" rotation="0  130 0"
              position="0 0 -2">
            </a-curvedimage>
```

50

```
        <a-curvedimage id="bc" src="#bc-place" transparent="true"
          height="2" radius="3" theta-length="40" rotation="0  80 0"
          position="0 0 -2">
        </a-curvedimage>

      <a-sky id="sky" src="Images/grid1.svg" color="rgb(200,200,200)"
      ></a-sky>
    </a-scene>

    <script>

        document.querySelector("#curhorseshoe").
        addEventListener('click', function() {
            document.getElementById("sky").
                setAttribute("src","Images/Horeshoe-Bend-PS.jpg");
        });

        document.querySelector("#atlantic").addEventListener('click',
        function() {
            document.getElementById("sky").
                setAttribute("src","Images/atlantic.jpg");
        });

        document.querySelector("#swit").addEventListener('click',
        function() {
            document.getElementById("sky").

                setAttribute("src","Images/switzerland.jpg");
        });

        document.querySelector("#bc").addEventListener('click',
        function() {
            document.getElementById("sky").
                setAttribute("src","Images/bc-place.jpg");
        });
    </script>
  </body>
</html>
```

This basic example of a content display web site explained how to use various entities and primitives in A-Frame. Feel free to experiment with different kinds of primitives and components (which will be discussed in Chapter 7) to understand how to use A-Frame better.

Summary

In this chapter, you learned how to build a basic "Hello, World" application in VR using A-Frame. You learned about bm-text-component and used the basic entities in a scene. Next, you learned how to build a basic content display web site from scratch where you used the curved image primitive as well as the camera entity. We also touched upon some basic JavaScript to implement additional interaction on the web site.

CHAPTER 6

Building a VR-Based Movie Theater

In this chapter, you will build the flagship application of this book, a VR movie theater. This will be an advanced application that will use components such as lighting and video display along with 3D models.

Planning the Movie Theater

First you have to plan the layout of your movie theater. Think about what your theater will look like and what different components will be present in the scene. You should choose these components carefully so as to give your movie theater a realistic look and feel. When you think of a movie theater, what comes to mind? A huge hall, big screen, chairs, speakers, pillars, and those exit signs glowing in the dark. In this chapter, you will be using Collada models, making use of three-dimensional models that are in .dae format. You will not have a roof on the theater and instead use a texture of a starry sky. You will also need textures for the walls and the floor. So, let's take a look at the finished scene to get some inspiration (Figure 6-1). You can view the demo online at http://drawvr.com/theater/.

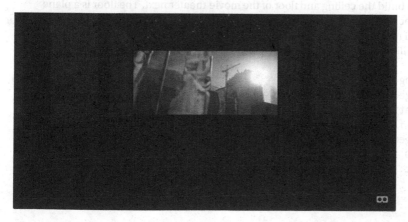

Figure 6-1. *The theater demo*

© Srushtika Neelakantam and Tanay Pant 2017
S. Neelakantam and T. Pant, *Learning Web-based Virtual Reality*,
DOI 10.1007/978-1-4842-2710-7_6

You can find the .dae models as well as the textures that have been used in the project in the code files on the Apress web site. However, the video file has not been provided, so you will have to download and link to your own .mp4 video file. Please note that currently YouTube embeds do not work with <a-video>.

Now let's get started building your virtual reality movie theater step by step. The following code includes meta tags for adding information about the author and for describing the web site for the search engines to spider through the page and give you better search engine optimization (SEO). You also include the aframe.min.js script.

```
<!DOCTYPE html>
<html>
  <head>
    <meta charset="utf-8">
    <title>Movie Theater WebVR Virtual Reality Experience Dying Light</title>
    <meta name="author" content="Donovan Kraeker">
    <meta name="description" content="A Movie Theater WebVR virtual reality
example website experience using A-Frame designed by Donovan Kraeker">
    <script src="aframe.min.js"></script>
  </head>
```

Next, start the <body> tag and the <a-scene> tag for your virtual reality environment. You define a new entity that is a camera and give it a default position. You also enable the look controls by setting enabled: true. Go ahead and hide the cursor by setting cursor-visible to enabled: false. Finally, set wasd-controls to enabled: true so that you can move around the movie theater to see the screen from different perspectives.

```
<body>
    <a-scene>
      <a-entity camera position="0 1.7 7.5" look-controls="enabled: true"
cursor-visible="enabled: false" wasd-controls="enabled: true"></a-entity>
```

You will build the ceiling and floor of the movie theater next. The floor is a plane that has a black texture. The ceiling is a box with the texture of stars so that it looks like an open-roof movie theater. Figure 6-2 shows the stars texture we have used for the example's ceiling.

```
<!-- Ceiling Floor -->
<a-entity geometry=" primitive: plane; height: 24; width: 22" position="0
0.5 2" rotation="-90 0 0" material="shader: flat; roughness: 1; src:
url(images/floor.jpg)"></a-entity>
<a-entity geometry=" primitive: box; depth: 0.1; height:24; width: 22"
position="0 12.5 2" rotation="-90 0 0" material="shader: standard; side:
bottom; src: url(images/stars.jpg)"></a-entity>
```

Figure 6-2. *Stars texture for ceiling*

You construct the front and back walls using the box geometry and set their heights and position. You set the color of these walls to black so that it emphasizes the dark setting of the room as is expected inside a movie theater when the movies are being shown.

```
<!-- Front Back Walls -->
<a-entity geometry=" primitive: box; depth: 0.1; height: 12; width: 22"
position="0 6.5 -10" material="shader: standard; color: #000"></a-entity>
<a-entity geometry=" primitive: box; depth: 0.1; height: 12; width: 22"
position="0 6.5 14" material="shader: standard; color: #000"></a-entity>
```

It's time to build the side walls for the movie theater. The side walls of the theater will be visible from the peripheral vision of the viewer at first glance. They shouldn't be too distracting and should complement the dark setting of the movie theater. You can use the same box geometries for the side walls and set the height, position, and rotation. In our example, we also set the roughness of the material to 1 and used the wall.jpg image as a texture, as shown in Figure 6-3.

```
<!-- Side Walls -->
<a-entity geometry=" primitive: box; depth: 0.1; height: 12; width: 24"
position="11 6.5 2" rotation="0 90 0" material="shader: standard; roughness:
1; src: url(images/wall.jpg)"></a-entity>
<a-entity geometry=" primitive: box; depth: 0.1; height: 12; width:
24" position="-11 6.5 2" rotation="0 90 0" material="shader: standard;
roughness: 1; src: url(images/wall.jpg)"></a-entity>
```

Figure 6-3. *Wall texture*

Now you will design the molding of the movie theater to improve its decor. You do so by using four box geometries and setting their dimensions, color, positions, rotation, and metalness.

```
<!-- Molding -->
<a-entity geometry=" primitive: box; depth: 0.5; height: 0.5; width: 24"
position="-10.75 0.5 2" rotation="0 90 0" material="shader: standard;
metalness: 0.5; color: #000"></a-entity>
<a-entity geometry=" primitive: box; depth: 0.5; height: 0.5; width: 24"
position="10.75 0.5 2" rotation="0 90 0" material="shader: standard;
metalness: 0.5; color: #000"></a-entity>
<a-entity geometry=" primitive: box; depth: 0.5; height: 0.5; width: 24"
position="-10.75 12.5 2" rotation="0 90 0" material="shader: standard;
metalness: 0.5; color: #000"></a-entity>
<a-entity geometry=" primitive: box; depth: 0.5; height: 0.5; width: 24"
position="10.75 12.5 2" rotation="0 90 0" material="shader: standard;
metalness: 0.5; color: #000"></a-entity>
```

You will now build the pillars for the left and right sides of the movie theater. You can do so by using the same box geometries that you have used before. You set their dimensions, positions, color, rotation, and metalness.

```
<!-- Pillars Left -->
<a-entity geometry=" primitive: box; depth: 0.5; height: 12; width: 1"
position="-10.8 6.5 -5" rotation="0 90 0" material="shader: standard;
metalness: 0.5; color: #000"></a-entity>
<a-entity geometry=" primitive: box; depth: 0.5; height: 12; width: 1"
position="-10.8 6.5 0" rotation="0 90 0" material="shader: standard;
metalness: 0.5; color: #000"></a-entity>
```

```
<a-entity geometry=" primitive: box; depth: 0.5; height: 12; width: 1"
position="-10.8 6.5 5" rotation="0 90 0" material="shader: standard;
metalness: 0.5; color: #000"></a-entity>
<a-entity geometry=" primitive: box; depth: 0.5; height: 12; width: 1"
position="-10.8 6.5 10" rotation="0 90 0" material="shader: standard;
metalness: 0.5; color: #000"></a-entity>

<!-- Pillars Right -->
<a-entity geometry=" primitive: box; depth: 0.5; height: 12; width: 1"
position="10.8 6.5 -5" rotation="0 90 0" material="shader: standard;
metalness: 0.5; color: #000"></a-entity>
<a-entity geometry=" primitive: box; depth: 0.5; height: 12; width: 1"
position="10.8 6.5 0" rotation="0 90 0" material="shader: standard;
metalness: 0.5; color: #000"></a-entity>
<a-entity geometry=" primitive: box; depth: 0.5; height: 12; width: 1"
position="10.8 6.5 5" rotation="0 90 0" material="shader: standard;
metalness: 0.5; color: #000"></a-entity>
<a-entity geometry=" primitive: box; depth: 0.5; height: 12; width: 1"
position="10.8 6.5 10" rotation="0 90 0" material="shader: standard;
metalness: 0.5; color: #000"></a-entity>
```

For building stool-like structures, you use the cylinder geometry and set its dimensions, metalness, and color. Please note that we have designed these stools to be closed by setting the open-ended attribute to false.

```
<!-- Stools -->
<a-entity geometry=" primitive: cylinder; radius: 0.2; height: 0.5"
position="10.7 9.5 -2.5" open-ended="false" material="shader: standard;
metalness: 0.5; color: #26030d"></a-entity>
<a-entity geometry=" primitive: cylinder; radius: 0.2; height: 0.5"
position="10.7 9.5 2.5" open-ended="false" material="shader: standard;
metalness:0.5; color: #26030d"></a-entity>
<a-entity geometry=" primitive: cylinder; radius: 0.2; height: 0.5"
position="10.7 9.5 7.5" open-ended="false" material="shader: standard;
metalness:0.5; color: #26030d"></a-entity>
<a-entity geometry=" primitive: cylinder; radius: 0.2; height: 0.5"
position="-10.7 9.5 -2.5" open-ended="false" material="shader: standard;
metalness:0.5; color: #26030d"></a-entity>
<a-entity geometry=" primitive: cylinder; radius: 0.2; height: 0.5"
position="-10.7 9.5 2.5" open-ended="false" material="shader: standard;
metalness:0.5; color: #26030d"></a-entity>
<a-entity geometry=" primitive: cylinder; radius: 0.2; height: 0.5"
position="-10.7 9.5 7.5" open-ended="false" material="shader: standard;
metalness:0.5; color: #26030d"></a-entity>
```

The speakers can just be black geometrical boxes that are perched high on the side walls of the movie theater.

```
<!-- Speakers -->
<a-entity geometry=" primitive: box; depth: 0.5; height: 1; width: 0.7"
position="10.5 9.5 -7.5" rotation="-10 90 0" material="shader: standard;
roughness: 0.7; color: #000"></a-entity>
<a-entity geometry=" primitive: box; depth: 0.5; height: 1; width: 0.7"
position="-10.5 9.5 -7.5" rotation="10 90 0" material="shader: standard;
roughness: 0.7; color: #000"></a-entity>
<a-entity geometry=" primitive: box; depth: 0.5; height: 1; width: 0.7"
position="10.5 9.5 12" rotation="-10 90 0" material="shader: standard;
roughness: 0.7; color: #000"></a-entity>
<a-entity geometry=" primitive: box; depth: 0.5; height: 1; width: 0.7"
position="-10.5 9.5 12" rotation="10 90 0" material="shader: standard;
roughness: 0.7; color: #000"></a-entity>
```

Security is one the most important considerations when designing closed halls like movie theaters. Let's make a small plane, position it along the side wall, and give it the texture of the door. Figure 6-4 shows the door texture that we have used in our code. Please note that it follows the same design aesthetics that we set for the textures.

```
<!-- Other -->
<a-entity geometry=" primitive: plane; height: 2; width: 1" position="5
1.5 13.93" material="shader: flat; side: back; transparent: true; src:
url(images/door.png)"></a-entity>
```

Figure 6-4. *Door texture*

Now, you need a glowing emergency exit sign so that the audience is able to see it in the dark in case of emergencies or when they need to hit the restroom after drinking too many cold drinks. So, make a plane and place it on a geometrical box. In this example, we are using the exit sign texture shown in Figure 6-5.

```
<a-entity geometry=" primitive: plane; height: 0.5; width: 0.6" position="5
3.5 13.93" material="shader: flat; side: back; transparent: true; src:
url(images/exit-sign.png)"></a-entity>
<a-entity geometry=" primitive: box; depth: 2; height: 16; width: 18"
position="0 2.8 -9.1" material="shader: standard; color: #000"></a-entity>
```

Figure 6-5. *Exit sign texture*

But wait, the theater isn't really complete until it actually shows a movie, right? Use the `<a-video>` tag to link to an existing video and set `autoplay` to `true` so that the video autoloads as soon as the scene loads. Set the width and height of the video display along with its position. Please note that you will have to edit the location and name of the video in the `src` attribute of the `<a-video>` tag. You can also add the three-dimensional model of a sofa by using a prebuilt three-dimensional `.dae` model. Finally, you add the sky using the `<a-sky>` tag and set its color to black. You then wrap up the virtual reality scene, body, and the HTML document itself.

```
<a-video src="videos/dying-light.mp4" autoplay="true" width="19" height="11"
position="0 5.5 -8"></a-video>
<a-model src="models/sofa.dae" scale="1 1 1" position="0 0.35 7.6"
rotation="0 90 0"></a-model>

    <!-- Lighting and background -->
    <a-sky color="#000"></a-sky>

  </a-scene>
 </body>
</html>
```

Your movie theater is now ready to be tested. Please note that this whole codebase might not work on your local system. You will need to make sure you are using a local web server or hosted web server with cross-origin resource sharing (CORS) with the correct MIME types rather than trying to use the filesystem. If you are loading the asset from a different domain, you will need CORS headers set on the asset. For some options, all resources hosted on GitHub Pages are served with CORS headers. (We will be discussing GitHub Pages as a deployment platform in the next chapter.) The scale of models is often very large as compared to the camera. The scale might be many times bigger than the user such that the user is inside the model and cannot see it. Try scaling it down to see where it is. The A-Frame inspector will help with this problem.

Building 3D Models with MagicaVoxel

MagicaVoxel (https://ephtracy.github.io) is a tool for building 3D scenes and models using voxels or blocks. MagicaVoxel makes modeling super easy, similar to building block-based structures in Minecraft. MagicaVoxel is available for both Windows and OS X. The best way to learn the MagicaVoxel is to play around with application controls and study the tooltips that show up when you hover your mouse over the various options.

After creating your model, you can export it to an A-Frame scene. This allows you to build custom models and use them in your virtual reality scenes. You can find a guide on using MagicaVoxel at https://aframe.io/docs/0.3.0/guides/building-with-magicavoxel.html.

Figure 6-6 shows the castle voxel made using MagicaVoxel.

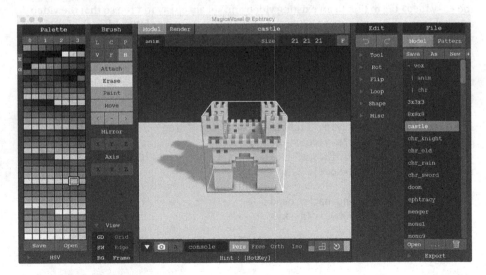

Figure 6-6. *Castle voxel*

Getting Prebuilt Models from Clara

Clara (`https://clara.io/`) is a web site that offers free three-dimensional models in many formats including the `.dae` format that you have been using for your scenes in this chapter. You can use the models that are available at this web site for use in your virtual reality scene. It is a pretty amazing site for obtaining complicated and realistic models for your WebVR application.

As an exercise, try building a virtual reality scene that displays a car showroom filled with cars of your choice.

Summary

In this chapter, you built the flagship application of this book, a VR movie theater. You built an advanced application that used components such as lighting and video display along with 3D models.

In the next chapter, you will learn about components in A-Frame and how to build them. You will also learn about the A-Frame registry, which hosts various components that have been built by the community. Finally, you will learn how to use these components in your WebVR scenes and enhance the quality of your scenes.

CHAPTER 7

■ ■ ■

A-Frame Components and the Registry

In this chapter, you will learn about A-Frame components and how to build them. Also, you will learn about the A-Frame registry that hosts various components that have been built by the community. Finally, you will learn how to use these components in your WebVR scenes and enhance the quality of your scenes without much effort at all.

A-Frame uses the entity-component system for managing the various objects in virtual reality scenes. Revisiting the definition of entity and components, an *entity* by itself does not exhibit any behavior, appearance, or functionality. An entity, however, can contain several *components*, and these components can impart characteristics to entities. Basically, components modify the entities that are the three-dimensional objects in virtual reality scenes. As an analogy, entities in the entity-component system are like classes in object-oriented programming, and components are like the methods of the class in which they exist.

The benefit of encapsulating most of the logic within components in A-Frame is that components become reusable and modular. This allows developers to share their code with others to use in their WebVR scenes.

Components in A-Frame

We'll now dive deeper to explain the components in A-Frame and how they are constructed. Components have properties that hold data. Components are registered using AFRAME.registerComponent. You pass a component name to register components and component definitions. Study the following example of the position component to understand how components are registered:

```
AFRAME.registerComponent('position', {
  schema: { type: 'vec3' },

  update: function () {
      var object3D = this.el.object3D;
      var data = this.data;
      object3D.position.set(data.x, data.y, data.z);
  }
});
```

© Srushtika Neelakantam and Tanay Pant 2017
S. Neelakantam and T. Pant, *Learning Web-based Virtual Reality*,
DOI 10.1007/978-1-4842-2710-7_7

A component has to define a schema, which in turn defines its properties. A component also has to define lifecycle methods, which handle what is to be done with the component's data. An important thing to note is that components in A-Frame have full access to three.js. In the previous example code, the position component has a vec3 value and is then applied to a three.js object called object3D.

The role of a component's schema is to define the component's properties. A component can have one property or several.

Lifecycle Methods of Components

The following sections cover the various lifecycle methods of components.

Component.init( )

The init( ) function is called just once in the lifecycle of the component, which is when it is attached to the entity.

Component.update( )

The update( ) function is called two or more times: once during the beginning of a component's lifecycle and then again every time the data of the component changes.

Component.remove( )

The remove( ) function is typically called when a component detaches itself from an entity.

Component.tick( )

The tick( ) function is called on every render loop of the scene, and it runs about 60 to 70 times per second.

Component.pause( ) and Component.play( )

The two functions pause( ) and play( ) are usually invoked when the component's entity calls these methods. One important thing to note is that whenever an entity either pauses or plays, all of its child entities will also follow the same behavior. These functions are usually implemented in scenarios where asynchronous properties are used, such as in the case of animations.

Built-in Components

Figure 7-1 shows some of the components that ship with A-Frame.

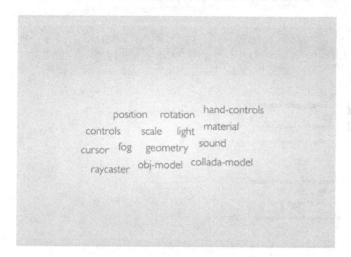

Figure 7-1. *A-Frame components*

A-Frame components are so easy to build and extensible that developers have built a large number of amazing components for use with A-Frame and have made them available to the community. Figure 7-2 shows the components built by the community in blue and the components shipped by A-Frame in red.

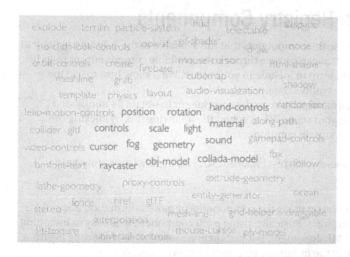

Figure 7-2. *Built-in and community-contributed components*

All the community-contributed components are available in the A-Frame registry (`https://aframe.io/aframe-registry/`), which is a curated collection of ready-to-use A-Frame components; the registry is also available from within the A-Frame inspector. The A-Frame team makes sure that the components work properly (Figure 7-3).

Figure 7-3. *Registry*

You can find lots of useful prebuilt components in the registry that you can include in your scenes to make them much more interesting with minimal effort. This is a good example of a tool fostering a healthy developer community, where advanced developers help new developers with their public contributions.

Using A-Frame Registry Components

We'll now discuss how to use the components that are available in the A-Frame registry in your virtual reality scenes. You can browse through the available components or search for the component that you want to include in your scene. We'll show how to use the mountain component in an empty scene.

First you click the download button on the component to obtain its minified JavaScript file to include in your scene. We reached the following link by clicking the download button on the mountain component:

```
https://unpkg.com/aframe-mountain-component@0.3.2/dist/aframe-mountain-
component.min.js
```

You can find instructions on using the components or more information about their properties on their GitHub pages. Basically, using each component is as easy as including a `<script>` tag in your HTML document. For instance, we inserted the following tag in our HTML document to use the mountain component in our example scene:

```
<script src="https://unpkg.com/aframe-mountain-component@0.3.2/dist/aframe-
mountain-component.min.js"></script>
```

The entire HTML code looks like this:

```
<html>
<head>
  <title>My A-Frame Scene</title>
  <script src="https://aframe.io/releases/0.3.0/aframe.min.js"></script>
  <script src="https://unpkg.com/aframe-mountain-component@0.3.2/dist/
aframe-mountain-component.min.js"></script>
</head>

<body>
  <a-scene>
        <a-mountain color="green"></a-mountain>
  </a-scene>
</body>
</html>
```

In the now available <a-mountain> tag, next set the color attribute to green so that it renders green hilly meadows. Just a single tag and the ready-made component accomplishes your task. Figure 7-4 shows how the scene looks in a browser.

Figure 7-4. *The hilly scene*

Other properties of the mountain component include the shadowColor attribute, which is used to diffuse the color of the mountain, and the sunPosition attribute, which allows you to set the position of the sun to shade the mountain.

As an exercise, try using different components from the A-Frame registry. Include them in your scenes and enhance the various scenes developed in the previous chapters. Also, try to implement the animation component for the clouds or water in your scene to make them look even more realistic. This will help you strengthen your skills using A-Frame and using its registry of ready-made components as well as make your life easier and simpler.

Summary

In this chapter, you learned about components in A-Frame and how to build them. You also learned that the A-Frame registry hosts various components that have been built by the developer community. Finally, you learned how to use these components in your WebVR scenes and easily enhance the quality of your scenes.

In the next chapter, we will cover how to use Git and GitHub to version control your application's code. That chapter will complement the knowledge that you have acquired over the course of reading this book.

CHAPTER 8

■ ■ ■

Version Control and Deploying Your Code on GitHub

In this chapter, you will learn about version control systems (VCSs) in general, as well as the most widely used VCS software, Git. You will also learn more about GitHub and use it to store your project files for further collaboration and updating. Following that, you will learn how to use your GitHub account to host your A-Frame projects for free using GitHub Pages.

Introduction to Version Control Systems

Try to picture being in an airplane just before landing. The crew broadcasts their reminders to put on your seat belt, put up the tray table, and open the window shades. The crew also tells you to save your work before closing your laptop if you've been working on it.

Thank you, flight crew! The work you do is probably precious to you, and therefore you will want to make sure your work is safely saved. It could be a disaster if something as big as a software project were lost because you forgot to save it or, worse, because of a system crash.

To help you avoid such scenarios, several version control systems are available. Version control systems are useful for developers and designers because they allow you to save and store each distinct version of your files. This allows you to roll back to any of the previous versions when you run into a problem in the current version. Thus, no project is completely lost because of errors, forgetfulness, or a crash.

VCSs are usually easy to use, providing a command-line prompt and a GUI interface for nondeveloper users. Another benefit of using a version control system is that several individuals can remotely collaborate on a single project without losing the integrity of the overall project and ensuring its stability. A software project is typically organized in a file tree structure, and the whole team works on different parts (files) of this project tree. They are continually updating, changing, deleting, and adding new source code or other resources to the project. All these version control issues are taken care of, by the VCS. In other words, each developer can work on his/her part of the project without disturbing or waiting for others. This is illustrated in Figure 8-1.

© Srushtika Neelakantam and Tanay Pant 2017
S. Neelakantam and T. Pant, *Learning Web-based Virtual Reality*,
DOI 10.1007/978-1-4842-2710-7_8

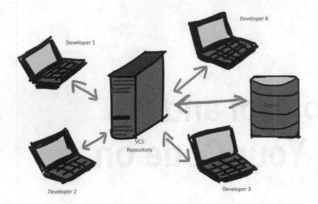

Figure 8-1. *A VCS*

Most of the good VCS applications are developer friendly in a way that they do not impose a particular workflow or methodology that might be different from a developer's usual working style. Most of them help developers make changes in the code without any hassle. They make sure not to let one developer's changes hinder the progress of other developers' work.

Advantages of Version Control

In the current world, it's hard to find software that is not built using version control. Doing this would be quite a risk. VCS is not only used in building software, but it facilitates the smooth introduction of new software developers into these teams.

Over the past couple of years, VCS has undergone a lot of improvements in terms of easy accessibility, security, and a lot of other aspects that make these applications more stable and safe to use. However, some VCS software outdoes others because of the specific benefits offered to the intended audience.

Version control systems can also be referred to as revision control systems (RCMs) or source code management (SCM). They all mean the same thing, so don't be overwhelmed if you hear one of these terms. Out of all the VCS applications, the one that is most widely used among organizations is called Git.

Git is open source, as are many other VCSs available today. You will learn more about Git in later sections. The following are the benefits of Git, which are also part of most other VCS applications too:

- *A stable long-term version history of every file in the project tree*: As discussed earlier, VCS applications allow you to save each version of every file in the project. This restricts the level that one person can screw up a project. At any point in time, you have the chance to roll back to the last stable version of a particular file. This also facilitates fixing bugs that are otherwise hard to find and fix. The versions of the files saved also contain certain meta information such as the author of the file, the last-changed date and time, the date created, and so on. Hence, in a highly collaborative environment, people are accountable only for what they do and do not need to take the blame for another developer's mistakes.

- *Branching and merging*: If teams were to work together, concurrently, on the same document, it would make absolutely no sense, and if the team members were to individually work, it would not really add to the progress of the collaborative project. Hence, VCS applications offer something called *branching*, which allows developers to use one of the multiple streams of the same file, hence facilitating them to work independently on whatever they are trying to implement. Later, when a stable portion of the implementation is complete, it can be merged with the main branch, often named the *master branch.*,

- *Traceability*: If all the team members are allowed to write, edit, and update the code, and solve bugs, it is equally important to be able to trace the changes made to those documents. VCSs have an interesting feature where they display both the previous and updated versions of the file in a color-coded format, highlighting the latest changes made. This can be crucial in order to solve some frequent bugs and work effectively even with legacy code. ,

Although there are many choices of VCS applications that can be used, in this chapter we'll focus on Git.

Git: All You Need to Know

Git, is the most widely used VCS application among software developers all over the world. Git has evolved through the years and has continuously received open source contributions. Originally Git was developed by the creator of the Linux operating system kernel, Linus Torvalds, in 2005.

Git today hosts an enormous number of software projects, both commercial as well as open source. Git essentially has a distributed architecture. What this means is that instead of having just a single central repository containing all the versions from the history of the development of a project, each developer who works on part of that project also has the copy of this "all versions history." Much of the popularity of Git is attributed to its distinct features, which are as follows:

- *Performance*: Git comes with strong performance characteristics. It focuses on the content on the files rather than on the names, which are mostly changed many times during the making of the project. The branching, merging, committing, and pushing of new versions of the document are all supported with the utmost efficiency and accuracy.

- *Security*: The repositories created on Git are safely secured using the SHA1 hashing algorithm for cryptography. Securing the repositories prevents unauthorized access to the contents. At any point in time, the complete version history is available for retrieval by authorized members who are duly authenticated. This is an important feature as opposed to some other VCS applications that have no or minimal security measures, which leads to a serious security breach within organizations.

- *Flexibility*: Git is truly flexible in the sense that it supports multiple development styles and methodologies. Git is compatible with existing protocols and systems. The level of version tracking available with Git has not been observed in any of its competitive counterparts.

Git vs. GitHub

While Git is the software that you install on your system that handles the version control for your files, GitHub is a place where you can store all your repositories. As its name suggests, it is a hub of Git repositories (*repos*), and it offers many other features.

Despite the clear differences between Git and GitHub, there still seems to be a lot of confusion about them from new developers. To clarify, Git is not just a hosting site; it is basically a collaboration tool where projects can be either public or private. Git is used for open source projects that are in the making and not complete already.

Installing Git on Your Machine

Here are the ways to install Git:

- *Linux*: Git allows Linux users to install the basic Git tools via a binary installer. You can do so with the help of any general package management tool that is usually preinstalled in your operating system. For instance, if you are on Fedora, you can use yum with the following command:

```
$sudo yum install git-all
```

- If you are Ubuntu, you can use the following command, which uses apt-get:

  ```
  $sudo apt-get install git-all
  ```

- *Mac*: Git can be installed on Mac in a variety of ways. As you might have guessed, the easiest way is to use the Xcode command-line tools. On Mac Mavericks (10.9) or above, you can try to run the git command on the terminal, and if the system doesn't have it installed already, it will prompt you to install it right there.

- *Windows*: Windows also gives you a couple of ways to install Git. The best way is to download the official build directly from the Git web site, which you can obtain from http://git-scm.com/download/win. Simply navigate to the particular web page and the download will start automatically. This project is called "Git for Windows," and it is separate from the actual Git project.

- An alternative way of installing Git on Windows includes installing GitHub for Windows. This package includes both the command-line version and the graphical user interface version of Git. This is particularly useful for nondeveloper users.

These instructions are directly sourced from the official Git documentation at https://git-scm.com/book/en/v2/Getting-Started-Installing-Git.

Working with GitHub

We'll now explain how to upload your A-Frame projects onto GitHub. The content provided here is limited to the example; providing the complete working details on GitHub is beyond the scope of this book.

As discussed earlier, GitHub provides an online collaboration tool as well as version control for all your projects. For this, you'll need to sign up for an account on GitHub and create repositories to store your projects. These repositories can be either private or public, depending on your account type. Here are the steps:

1. Create a GitHub account.

   Head over to https://github.com and sign up for an account (Figure 8-2). Initially, when you are hosting small projects, you can go for a free account, which is public. (Remember, A-Frame is open source.)

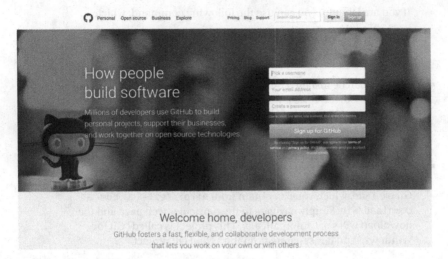

Figure 8-2. *GitHub*

2. Create a new repository.

   After you are logged in to your account, click the "New repository" button. The window in Figure 8-3 will be displayed. Add the name of your repo, which is public by default, for a free account.

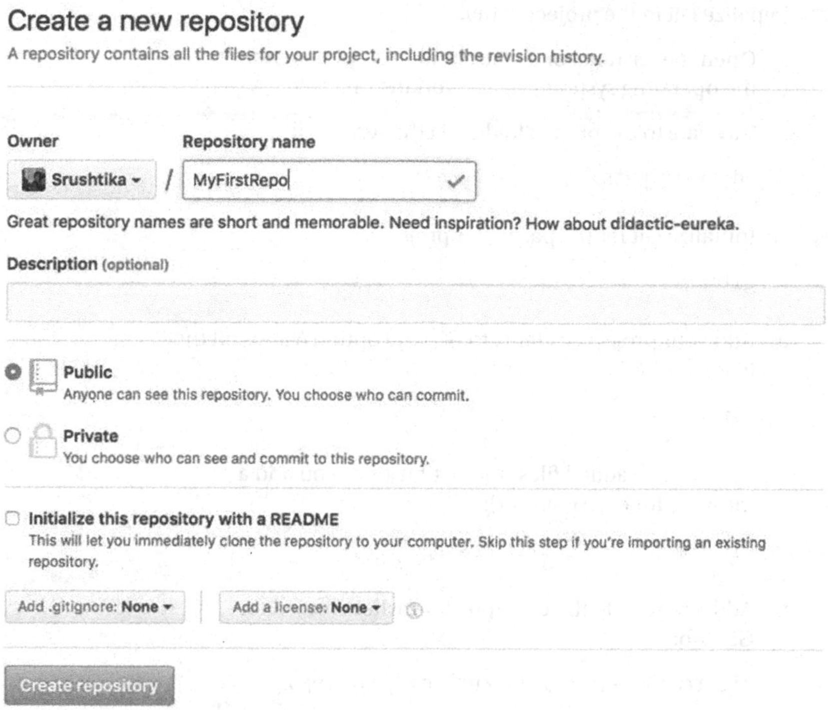

Create a new repository

A repository contains all the files for your project, including the revision history.

Owner   Repository name

Srushtika ▾ /   MyFirstRepo   ✓

Great repository names are short and memorable. Need inspiration? How about **didactic-eureka.**

Description (optional)

○ ▦ **Public**
      Anyone can see this repository. You choose who can commit.

○ 🔒 **Private**
      You choose who can see and commit to this repository.

☐ **Initialize this repository with a README**
   This will let you immediately clone the repository to your computer. Skip this step if you're importing an existing repository.

Add .gitignore: **None ▾** | Add a license: **None ▾** ⓘ

Create repository

Figure 8-3. *Adding a repository name*

A repository. is like a folder inside which you store all files related to the particular project. You can choose to initialize the repo with a README; this is nothing but an additional text file where you'll later add details about the project for someone else to understand or for yourself to revisit.

3. Initialize Git in the project folder.

    a. Open the terminal or a command prompt depending on the operating system you are working on.

    b. Navigate to the project folder via the terminal:

```
cd <file path>
```

    c. Initialize Git for the particular project:

```
git init
```

    d. Add your project contents to Git (the option A adds all the files):

```
git add -A
```

    e. Commit the added files (the option m lets you add a message for each commit):

```
git commit -m "Commit Message"
```

    f. Add a remote to the Git repo you earlier created on GitHub:

```
git remote add origin <url of your repo>
```

    g. The URL of your repo is available after you've created a new repo, as shown in Figure 8-4.

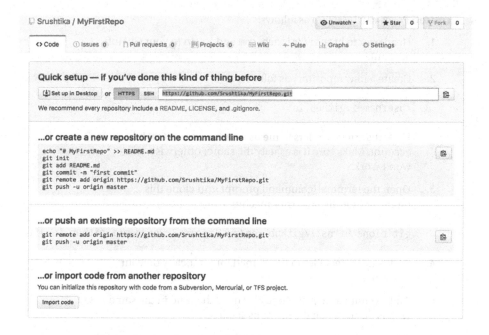

Figure 8-4. *URL for repo*

> h. Push the committed files to your GitHub repo:
>
> ```
> git push origin master
> ```

The commit command essentially traces the changes in the project, whereas the push command uploads the updated project to your repo.

Hosting Your VR Web Site for Free Using GitHub Pages

GitHub Pages is a service provided to GitHub users to allow static hosting of their sites directly from their repositories. Currently, GitHub allows a single site per account for a personal user. These sites are publicly available for anyone to view even if the particular repo is a private one from a paid account. Hence, care must be taken in such cases so as not to reveal sensitive information that might cause a privacy/security breach for your organization. GitHub recommends not using GitHub Pages to retrieve users' sensitive information such as passwords or credit card numbers via forms on the web site.

Although the GitHub Pages service comes with a few terms and conditions, we are good to go using it for the basic A-Frame VR applications.

GitHub Pages can be set up as follows:

1. Head over to https://github.com and log in to your GitHub account.

2. Create a new repository as follows:

   <username>.github.io

   Here <username> refers to the username of your GitHub account. Make sure it is exactly the same; otherwise, this won't work.

3. Open the terminal/command prompt and clone this repository locally onto your machine.

   git clone https://github.com/<username>/<username>.github.io.git

4. Add your project files to this cloned folder locally on your machine.

5. Add, commit and push these files onto the repo in the same way as discussed in the previous section.

6. After this, head over to your GitHub repository and navigate to the Settings tab (Figure 8-5).

Figure 8-5. *Settings tab on GitHub*

7. Scroll down until you reach the GitHub Pages section (Figure 8-6). In that, choose the branch (master) and click Save.

GitHub Pages

✓ Your site is published at https://srushtika.github.io/

GitHub Pages is designed to host your personal, organization, or project pages from a GitHub repository.

Source

Your GitHub Pages site is currently being built from the master branch. Learn more.

| master branch ▾ | Save |

User pages must be built from the master branch.

Custom domain

Custom domains allow you to serve your site from a domain other than srushtika.github.io. Learn more.

| | Save |

Overwrite site

Replace your existing site by using our automatic page generator. Author your content in our Markdown editor, select a theme, then publish.

| Launch automatic page generator |

☑ **Enforce HTTPS** — Required for your site because you are using the default domain (srushtika.github.io)
HTTPS provides a layer of encryption that prevents others from snooping on or tampering with traffic to your site. When HTTPS is enforced, your site will only be served over HTTPS. Learn more.

***Figure 8-6.** GitHub Pages section*

Your site is now live, and you can use it to host your VR web site (or any other web site) for free on GitHub. So, every other repository you add can be hosted under this URL. For instance, if you have another repository named mywebvr that has the file Hello World, which in turn has an index.html file, this file will be available on GitHub Pages at the following URL:

https://srushtika.github.io/mywebvr/Hello%20World/index.html

For a virtual reality scene, the first thing you want to do after having developed it is to try it in your smartphone fixed in a VR headset. However, it can be tedious to host your virtual reality scene if you don't own a domain already, even if it is just for testing purposes. Hence, in this particular case, GitHub Pages is a great service.

In addition, any minute changes to the code can be made directly in the hosted version of the document in your GitHub account. This is another quite helpful feature.

Summary

In this chapter, you learned about version control systems and their advantages. You also learned about Git, which is the most common VCS application. You also looked at how to install it on a local system. After reviewing the difference between Git and GitHub, you learned to use GitHub to upload your projects from your machine to the GitHub repos. Finally, you looked at GitHub Pages and how to use the service to host your own web sites for free.

Index

A

A-Frame, 6
  components and registry, 63
    built-in, 65–66
    lifecyclemethods (*see* Lifecycle methods of components, A-Frame)
    position component, 63
    schema, 64
    using, 66–67
  inspector, 7
  online editor, 8
A-Frame library, 17
  basic application, 18–19
  ECS, 20
    caching assets to improve performance, 21
    components and building blocks, 21–22
    Kevin's illustration, 20
    mixins, 21
  example, 18
  inspector, 35
    components panel, 37–38
    scene graph, 36
    viewport, 36–37
  key features, 19
  primitives, 22
    <a-box>, 22–23
    <a-camera>, 23
    <a-circle>, 24–25
    <a-collada-model>, 25–26
    <a-cone>, 26
    <a-cursor>, 23
    <a-curvedimage>, 26–27
    <a-cylinder>, 27
    <a-dodecahedron>, 28
    <a-image>, 28
    <a-light>, 29
    <a-obj-model>, 29
    <a-octahedron>, 30
    <a-plane>, 30
    <a-ring>, 31
    <a-sky>, 31–32
    <a-sound>, 32
    <a-sphere>, 32
    <a-tetrahedron>, 33
    <a-torus>, 33
    <a-torus-knot>, 34
    <a-video>, 34
    <a-videosphere>, 35
AFRAME.registerComponent, 63
A-Painter, 15

B

Boilerplate code, 19

C

Clara, prebuilt models, 61
Computer-based VR setup, 2
Constellation sensors, Oculus Rift, 13
Content delivery network (CDN), 18
Controllers, Oculus Rift, 13
Cross-origin resource sharing (CORS), 60

D

3D Collada models, 25
Developer tools, WebVR, 6
  A-Frame, 6
  Vizor, 8
  WebVR-Boilerplate, 8
3D models with MagicaVoxel, 60

■ E, F

Entity-component system (ECS), 20
    caching assets to improve
        performance, 21
    components and building
        blocks, 21–22
    Kevin's illustration, 20
    mixins, 21

■ G

Git
    benefits, 71
    features, 71–72
    Git *vs.* GitHub, 72
    to install, 72
        Linux, 72
        Mac, 73
        Windows, 73
Git for Windows, 73. *See also* Git
GitHub
    features, 73
    Git *vs.* GitHub, 72
    working with, 73
        creating GitHub account, 73
        creating new repository, 74–75
        GitHub pages, 77–78
        GitHub pages section, 79
        initialize Git in project
            folder, 76–77
        settings tab on GitHub, 78
Google Cardboard, 11–13
Graphical user interface (GUI), 35

■ H, I, J, K

"Hello, World" VR application, 39
    bm-font-text-component, 39–40
    understanding the flow, 40–45
HTC Vive, 14

■ L

Lifecycle methods of components,
    A-Frame
    init() function, 64
    pause() and play() function, 64
    remove() function, 64
    tick() function, 64
    update() function, 64

■ M, N

MagicaVoxel, 3D models with, 60
Mixins, 21
Mobile-based VR setup, 2
Movie theater, VR, 53
    <a-scene> tag, 54
    <a-video> tag, 59
    <body> tag, 54
    box geometry, 55–56
    CORS, 60
    cylinder geometry, 57
    .dae models, 54
    demo, 53
    door texture, 58
    exit sign texture, 59
    security, 58
    SEO, 54
    side walls, 55–56
    speakers, 57–58
    stars texture, 54–55
MozVR, definition, 6

■ O

Oculus Rift device, 13

■ P

Pretzel-shaped model, 34
Primitives, 22
    <a-box>, 22–23
    <a-camera>, 23
    <a-circle>, 24–25
    <a-collada-model>, 25–26
    <a-cone>, 26
    <a-cursor>, 23
    <a-curvedimage>, 26–27
    <a-cylinder>, 27
    <a-dodecahedron>, 28
    <a-image>, 28
    <a-light>, 29
    <a-obj-model>, 29
    <a-octahedron>, 30
    <a-plane>, 30
    <a-ring>, 31
    <a-sky>, 31–32
    <a-sound>, 32
    <a-sphere>, 32
    <a-tetrahedron>, 33
    <a-torus>, 33

<a-torus-knot>, 34
<a-video>, 34
<a-videosphere>, 35

■ Q

Quake 3 WebGL Demo, 16

■ R

Repository, 75
Revision control systems (RCMs).
        See Version control system, 70

■ S, T, U

Search engine optimization (SEO), 54
sphericalEnvMap, 42

■ V

Version control systems
    advantages, 70
    applications, 70
    benefits, 69
    features, 69
    Git, 71
Virtual reality (VR)
    content display web site, 45
        <a-curved-image> primitive, 45
        a-scene tag, 45–46
        camera entity, 47–48
        cursor to be ring shape, 47–48
        event listener, 49
        example, 50–51
        images as assets, 46
    definition, 1
    devices
        popular devices, 4
        Samsung Gear VR, 4
    hardware setup, types, 2
        computer-connected, 2
        mobile-based, 2
    movietheater (see VR movie theater)
    usage, 1

Vizor, 8
    Build mode, 9
    editor window, 8
VR movie theater, 53
    <a-scene> tag, 54
    <a-video> tag, 59
    <body> tag, 54
    box geometry, 55–56
    CORS, 60
    cylinder geometry, 57
    .dae models, 54
    demo, 53
    door texture, 58
    exit sign texture, 59
    security, 58
    SEO, 54
    side walls, 55–56
    speakers, 57–58
    stars texture, 54–55

■ W, X, Y, Z

Web-based virtual reality, 3
WebVR
    applications
        current state, 4
        opportunities, 3
    mailing list, 5
    projects, 11
        A-Painter, 15
        Blair Witch WebVR
            experience, 15
        Google Cardboard, 11–13
        HTC Vive, 14
        Oculus Rift, 13
        Quake 3 WebGL Demo, 16
        requirements, 14
        VR mode, 13
    Slack, 5
WebVR API
    definition, 5
    features, 6
    purpose-built interfaces, 5
WebVR-Boilerplate, 8

Get the eBook for only $4.99!

Why limit yourself?

Now you can take the weightless companion with you wherever you go and access your content on your PC, phone, tablet, or reader.

Since you've purchased this print book, we are happy to offer you the eBook for just $4.99.

Convenient and fully searchable, the PDF version enables you to easily find and copy code—or perform examples by quickly toggling between instructions and applications.

To learn more, go to http://www.apress.com/us/shop/companion or contact support@apress.com.

Printed in the United States
By Bookmasters